FIRST-TIME LANDLORD-HOUSE RENTAL PREP BOOK

THE LANDLORD'S ESSENTIAL GUIDE TO GETTING IT RIGHT FIRST TIME-BECOME AN AUTOPILOT LANDLORD

J. M. SARSFIELD

To request permissions, contact the publisher at info@strikepublishing.com.

First paperback edition: April 2022

Published by: Strike Publishing

Website: strikepublishing.com

CONTENTS

The Energy Crisis Has Guaranteed A Damp Assault On UK Rental Properties In Winter 2022 / 2023!!

READ THIS BOOKLET:

To Understand The Different Types Of Damp

To Find Out Why **Condensation Damp** Is **The Insidious Saboteur!!**

To Understand How **Condensation Damp - The Most Difficult Type Of Damp** Can Be Stopped In Its Tracks By Planning Ahead.

BUT

YOU NEED TO START NOW BEFORE **AUTUMN 2022**

You Need To **Plan Ahead NOW:-**

- If You Want To **Prevent Tenant Complaints**
- If You Want To **Avoid Substantial Remediation Costs**
- If You Want To **Maintain Your Property Asset Value**

Use the QR Code or The Link below To Receive Your Bonus Copy Of Damp The Saboteur condensationmanagement.jamessarsfield.strikepublishing.com

JAMES SARSFIELD
GORDON DREW

INTRODUCTION

The reason I wrote this book for new landlords is that I continue to see individuals who think that they can rent out a property, engage a managing agent, or put-up a 'To Let' board and just wait for a new tenant to roll up without any preparation or forward planning to eliminate or prepare for technical issues in the property.

I have been involved in the property sector as a landlord and actively working with landlords for 10 years. The thoughts and recommendations that I express in this book are based on my experiences, as well as those of colleagues, landlords, and trade professionals with whom I have worked.

Forgive my emphatic writing approach at times but it still amazes me that a house rental is often not treated as a business decision, which it is, regardless of the reason to rent a property out. The lack of attention to detail in letting preparation is effectively poor management in what is possibly the most significant business decision most rental property owners make.

I regularly hear about landlords facing issues during the tenancy that could have been prevented if they had planned ahead. In the early days of my rental business, I made rookie mistakes and now I look back and wish there had been a handbook or two to guide me in reducing the risk of the foreseeable issues that arose during the tenancies.

Recently I heard of a landlord who rented out his family property to students. He received a call from the managing agent a few weeks after the tenants moved in, to advise there had been an uncontrollable leak from a bathroom sink tap.

There was no internal stop tap in the house and no isolator valve to the damaged tap.

It took the agent nearly two hours to get a plumber to the location.

The result was damage to the bathroom flooring, kitchen cabinets, kitchen worktop, and kitchen flooring to the value of nearly £2,000.

The landlord had not taken out any property or landlord's insurance but had been planning to do so!

In my discussion with the managing agent, it was clear that the landlord had not been advised about installing a stop tap or tap isolation valves. These could all have been installed at a relatively low cost.

I would say that the landlord had not been served well by the agent's property management team but also should have thought through the potential risks himself and planned more effectively, prior to the rental. A stop tap serving the property would have been enough to prevent the excessive damage.

This book will help you to prepare your rental property and plan maintenance tasks during the tenancy, taking account of current legal and safety obligations that are becoming more onerous for landlords.

If certain maintenance works are not carried out or planned prior to the tenancy, then issues that arise during the tenancy tend to become reactive. This can increase the repair costs, especially if they become critical and occur out-of-hours.

I understand there is a budget to consider, so you need to think about what is critical now and what should be planned. This will be specific to each property.

Not doing this preparation will lead to headaches later. Why? Because you will be remote from the property. You will receive phone calls from the tenant for reactive repairs. If you have a managing agent they will react to repair requests but may not be adept at assisting you to plan how to manage your property asset for ongoing planned maintenance.

Had you prepared, it is very possible that you could have carried out those works at a lesser cost prior to the rental or planned them in during the rental.

Once you have read this book you will be in a better position to effectively manage the physical elements of your property rental before your first tenant arrives and have a good idea of what to plan for during the tenancy. The aim of this book is to cover buy-to-lets, a property purchased to rent out, an accidental rental from an inheritance, or an ex-family home.

This book will highlight what you should consider before you rent out your property and what you may want to plan for during your first tenancy.

I will walk you through the different aspects of a typical rental property and highlight the areas you may want to consider.

This book is structured by maintenance categories or property areas. For each category I go through suggested pre-tenancy preparations, suggested timelines for completion, potential pitfalls to look out for, tips to ensure tenant satisfaction, and ideas to achieve a cost-effective approach to maintaining your rental property over the long term.

Look out for the summaries at the end of each chapter to assist with your maintenance planning.

Please remember that your rental property is a business whether you are an accidental landlord through inheritance, a buy-to-let, or you are letting your old family home or building a property portfolio. Decisions should be made on a business basis using the tenancy agreement as a framework. Issues will arise that may need negotiation with the tenant.

Finally, I sincerely hope that you gain some ideas to assist you with managing the physical elements of your property rental. Thank you.

1

LANDLORD VS TENANT VS HOUSEHOLDER RESPONSIBILITIES

You will see mention of householder responsibility later within the book. This is because I believe there are three stakeholder positions in the domestic property rental relationship. The landlord who owns or leases the property and rents it out, the tenant who rents the property, and as it is also their home, they are also the householder.

As the property is the tenant's home, they have householder responsibilities which means they need to manage certain areas just as they would if they purchased their own property.

I am not talking about fixing guttering or resolving weather-related leaks or even updating the decoration as these are included in the tenancy agreement as the landlord's responsibility. A landlord should maintain his asset. I am talking about areas such as not putting fats down drains. Not flushing wet wipes down the toilet. Ensuring window sills are wiped down to clear moisture before the moisture mixes with airborne mould spores and produces black mould spots. Not drying clothes indoors on an airer without opening windows to allow for adequate ventilation. Clearing leaves from ground drains before they cause drain blockages. Keeping shrubs trimmed back so they don't become a nuisance to the public on pavements or next-door neighbours. Overloading an extension lead with too many electrical items causing the socket to fail. I could go on!

I think this is a 'common sense' concept that, as a landlord, you may want to keep in mind as you start your property rental journey.

Some issues that arise will be the tenant's responsibility and some will be yours. Then there is a grey area. The issues where some common sense needs to be applied and responsibility taken by the appropriate party. If you are working with a managing agent, be ready to discuss issues where you feel responsibility should fall to the tenant and not you as the landlord. I mention this as some managing agents recruit personnel to handle maintenance issues who are not familiar with the finer points of tenancy agreements, and they may pass you a repair issue to consider as if you are automatically responsible. If you are not familiar with renting you may think that the managing agent must have their assessment correct and the area passed to you is your responsibility. That may not always be the case.

Should you manage the property yourself, be ready to challenge your tenants on whose responsibility an issue may be. Some landlords are uncomfortable with this type of situation as they feel it may affect their relationship with the tenant. Stop! If they come to you with an issue that, on common-sense grounds, you feel may be their duty to resolve, advise accordingly.

For instance, issues such as modern waterproof-rated light units for bathroom areas come around time and again. Tenants claim that they can't source the light bulbs. The fact is they may not have realised that these are readily available from high street and online retailers. The only time a landlord may want to get involved is when a light fitting is on a ceiling that is too high to safely reach on a standard stepladder. In this case, on health and safety grounds, it is recommended that the landlord carry out this task.

To help you feel more comfortable about tackling these types of situations, think through the risks of confronting the tenant about appropriate responsibility.

If you are afraid of losing a tenant but you feel it is right to challenge a reported issue they think you should pay for, then think through the probability of them leaving. The tenant would need to find a new home, pay a new deposit, suffer possible deposit loss for repairs to your property, plus moving expenses. A lot for them to think about.

At the end of the day, a tenancy is a business relationship and you should treat it as such; not always thinking you have to keep the tenant happy at any cost. Obviously, you want to keep your customer happy, but it is reasonable for both sides to accept they have a duty to contribute to a successful relationship.

There seems to be an ongoing shift in expectations from tenants. This is a personal opinion but I have seen an increasing number of illustrations of this shift as I talk to people in the industry. Tenants seem to be more demanding and areas that would traditionally be accepted as tenant responsibility appear to be increasingly more fluid. I have a gut feel that 'googling' by tenants sometimes drives their 'knowledge' of issues and likely causes and they then build their case based on this information. Some common-sense thinking by landlords or property management staff needs to be applied in league with access to the tenancy agreement.

LANDLORD VS TENANT VS HOUSEHOLDER RESPONSIBILITIES SUMMARY

There are three elements to a rental. The traditional landlord and tenant relationship plus the tenant as a householder where the responsibilities align with those of a house owner or mortgagee.

Beware of this relationship and when issues arise that are not covered within the tenancy agreement, apply common sense to help work out who is the responsible party.

NOTES

2

TENANCY AGREEMENT

A formal tenancy agreement is not legally required, however, certain information is required to be shared with the tenant in writing. A tenancy agreement based on a template is the best vehicle to provide this information. This is also a good foundation on which to add additional information about how the tenancy will run, who is responsible for different issues, and what responsibilities you want the tenant to take on as a householder.

If you are working with a managing agent they will have a standard agreement and you can ask that other elements be included that will tailor the agreement to your specific rental property.

The government has a model shorthold tenancy agreement that can be downloaded and used as a template.

If you are managing the property yourself, use a good quality agreement template from an accredited landlord organisation.

You should be clear about what you expect from the tenant in terms of reporting repairs as they arise and who will be responsible for those repairs. Beware, it is probably better that you consider taking responsibility for all repairs even if the tenant is ultimately responsible for the cost, to ensure the quality of the work meets your standards.

Two examples of agreement inclusions could be:

Redecoration. It is worth including that the tenant can redecorate with the landlord's permission. The work should be in line with the current decoration to prevent a situation of the tenant restyling in a manner that would make it difficult to re-let in the future.

Upkeep of external areas. If the property has a garden area then be clear in the agreement who is responsible for the upkeep.

As tenancy agreements differ across publishers and managing agents, include an addendum that allows you to add extra terms you want to include in the agreement. Consider the government's shorthold tenancy agreement template.

TENANCY AGREEMENT SUMMARY

This is an important document to be included as part of your rental. Use this as a base for the legal and commercial elements such as rent and responsibilities. Use an addendum to enable additional terms to be included in the basic agreement.

Do not run your tenancy without a written agreement even if it is not a legal requirement.

Email exchanges documenting rental information are difficult to manage.

Verbal agreements even less so!

NOTES

3

INVENTORIES

An inventory is a crucial document associated with the tenancy agreement to prove the state of the property and any included items such as fixtures and fittings, furniture, and appliances at the tenancy start and end dates.

The inventory is second only to the tenancy agreement in terms of importance.

This documents the property details, a snapshot of the state of the property, the landlord-supplied contents, and their condition at check-in and then again at check-out.

It is best to have the tenant present when you, the managing agent, or an inventory intermediary carries out this process as some of the inclusions may be subjective and require discussion. Make sure the inventory is carried out before any of the tenant's possessions are moved in to prevent any confusion on any photos taken of what is included in the tenancy.

The tenant will be equally interested in the inventory as this prevents them from being charged when they leave the property for issues that existed prior to check-in.

The inventory and periodic inspections can help you to benchmark the physical property status and help you to put in place a maintenance plan to keep the property in a good state over the period that it is under tenancy. If you are not local to the property and cannot visit and instead rely on third parties to inspect and carry out check-ins and check-outs, inventories and inspection reports can be a valuable report tool.

Recently I was involved in an inspection analysis of a property where the property management changed hands between managing agents. The landlord was on a long-term assignment abroad. The check-in inventory was presented to the landlord and he was shocked at the state of the garden, boundary fences, and walls. There had been no inspection carried out for 3 years since the incumbent tenant moved in. The landlord engaged a solicitor to file a claim against the former managing agent for negligence related to the management of his property. Regular inspection reports could have prevented this situation arising.

Inventories can also assist with issues such as damp claims that can often turn out to be condensation damp, sometimes caused by living conditions. An adjudicator will have an agreed documentary snapshot of the property prior to the issue arising to assist with the deliberations.

The inventory reports are important for both the landlord and the tenant. Both have an interest in having the property contents and condition documented for future reference. The two reports at check-in and check-out will clearly show how the property has changed during the tenancy.

Inventories need to be clear, include photographs, be easy to read, and should be an accurate reflection of the condition of the property.

Remember, a well-documented inventory will be an excellent operational tool for when repair requests are raised to ensure you replace like with like to keep your budget in check.

Also, at inspections and at the end of the tenancy, it will be useful to have this information to ensure you, as a landlord, do not have to pay for repairs that are not your responsibility.

The inventories should be checked by the tenant at both check-in and check-out and be countersigned by them. This will reduce the likelihood of any dispute on a valid claim on the deposit, especially if you have to use a mediator who will want documentary evidence to assist in the decision-making process.

The area that causes controversy at the end of the tenancy is what is fair wear and tear versus wilful neglect or damage. This must, in the first instance come down to discussion between the landlord and the tenant or the managing agent and the tenant. If there is a difference of opinion then the Deposit Service will provide an adjudication service to assist in reaching an agreement.

NOTES

4

INSPECTIONS

Inspections should be carried out periodically to enable you to check the status of the property and be confident it is being managed as agreed by the tenant.

Inspections can be carried out by you as the landlord, the managing agent, or a nominated third party.

This opportunity can be used to check the tenant's living conditions, check for maintenance issues, check for illegal activities, and check compliance with the tenancy agreement such as the number of persons residing at the property. It is also an opportunity to review any external areas, especially those that border neighbouring properties. Property border disputes related to overgrown hedging, shrubs, and trees are quite common. Also, as you have a duty of care to ensure you provide a safe letting, it will give you an opportunity to determine if there are any safety issues that require attention that have not already been reported by the tenant.

The law dictates you need to give at least 24 hours' notice to enter the property and you will also need to agree to an appointment at a reasonable time of day unless you are attending an emergency.

If a third party is to access the property, the tenant has the right to ask for written notice of this access request.

This is your property but it is also the tenant's home, so think about how you would like to be treated if access was required to your home.

Taking photos at inspections is an important part of managing the property. Some tenants are resistant because you may incidentally include some of their personal possessions. To avoid this conflict, include the fact that you will be taking photographs when you send your appointment letter, email, or text or on the arrangement phone call so they have an opportunity to put away any sensitive possessions. When you take photos ask the tenant if there is anything they want to remove from the area to be photographed. Be careful to restrict the photos to ones that will record the state of the property, any issues that need attention, and ones that illustrate how the tenant is managing the property.

INVENTORY AND INSPECTIONS SUMMARY

Both of these elements are important. The check-in and check-out inventories are major asset management documents. Inspections are operational documents that help you manage the property, and the tenants' management of your property, during a tenancy.

My strong recommendation is to be consistent with your inspections so the tenant knows they will happen at set intervals. If it is needed, this will help the tenant understand that they need to adhere to the spirit of the tenancy agreement throughout the tenancy.

NOTES

5

CERTIFICATIONS

ELECTRICAL INSTALLATION CONDITION REPORT (EICR)

Electrical Installation Condition Reports were brought into law in April 2020. These require you, as a landlord, to have the fixed wiring system in the property checked every 5 years to ensure it meets the current standards and to also check the integrity of the system. The following areas are checked as part of the test: sockets, light fittings, cabling, and the consumer unit (fuse board). If you have not rented out the property to date, then this is one area that you will need to have checked prior to your first rental, along with the gas safety check.

One area of debate that comes up time and again is plastic consumer units. Many current domestic installations have plastic consumer units which were considered safe for many years. These are no longer considered best practice under current regulations due to potential fire risk but they have not been outlawed. As long as they can house all the required circuit breakers, they are still acceptable. Discuss the reasons given by your electrician if the issue of a replacement unit is raised. Just remember, as part of risk reduction it may be better to invest in a metal consumer unit. If an incident were to happen and the consumer unit was the source of the fire, then the fact that it was not changed may have a negative effect on your defence.

Once you have the 5-year electrical certificate, you must give your tenant a copy at check-in along with the current gas safety certificate.

ANNUAL GAS SAFETY CHECK

If there is a gas boiler in the rental property, your new tenant will need to have a copy of the current gas safety certificate as required by law. This means that you should employ a gas service engineer to check the integrity of the boiler and associated parts as well as any other gas appliance and issue a certificate to the tenant on the first day of the tenancy.

This gas safety check needs to be undertaken on an annual basis as part of the overall check of the gas system in the house. It does not check the effectiveness of the boiler or that of the central heating system.

- The main areas covered by the annual gas safety check are:
- The integrity of the gas flue and associated pipes and vents;
- That the gas safety devices are working correctly;
- That there is suitable air supply to the appliance;
- That the appliance is stable in its location and is connected to the mains gas supply; and
- That the burners are burning correctly in the boiler or other gas appliances.

When an engineer carries out an annual gas check they will send you the certificate by email or post. You should provide your tenant with a copy within 28 days of the completed check.

As a landlord you will need a copy of this certificate and the law requires that you keep it for 2 years.

If you are working with a managing agent, they will ensure, as part of their business process, that their gas contractors submit certificate copies to them once a gas check is carried out on your rental property. These are usually kept on file in case of a Gas Safe audit on your rental property and a copy given to the tenant.

For planning purposes, a landlord can have the safety check carried out up to 2 months early and still retain the original annual safety check date. For instance if the gas safety check is due June 1st you may have it carried out on April 2nd and still retain the next year's check date as June 1st.

ENERGY PERFORMANCE CERTIFICATE (EPC)

An Energy Performance Certificate is as important as its electrical installation condition certificate and annual gas certificate counterparts.

An EPC is a measure of the energy efficiency of the property and will give information on the energy usage and costs as well as suggest improvements that will contribute to energy and cost savings. Once attained, it is valid for 10 years.

The number of landlords who do not understand the significance of Energy Performance Certification is incredibly high.

Please be aware that if you try to market a property for rent and you have not attained an EPC that meets the current standard (currently C for most individual properties), then you could be fined up to £4,000.

Trading Standards police the system and there are strict measures in place that prevent landlords from reaching the point of being fined if you are working through a managing agent. If you are managing your own property you need to employ an assessor and take appropriate action to attain the required certification.

Tenants are more aware of the legal responsibilities of landlords and know that they need to be handed the latest annual gas certificate, the electrical test certificate, and the latest Energy Performance Certificate.

So, what do the various ratings mean and what measures are available to assist you in moving up the scale?

First, the property needs to be assessed. This entails a visit by an approved assessor who will carry out an energy assessment survey.

An energy assessment will rate the property at a particular grade of between A and G. A property with a Grade A is the most energy efficient with the lowest energy costs and G as the most energy inefficient.

Before an assessment takes place, I recommend you work on low-cost elements that can have a positive effect to ensure you are aiming towards the permissible grading of E or above.

The DIY elements to enhance your EPC rating are:

- Change light bulbs for LEDs;
- Increase the loft insulation to between 220mm to 270mm. 220mm for cellulose, 250 for rockwool and 270 for glass wool (new building regulation requirements);
- Close off any non-working fireplaces;
- Draught-proof windows and doors where necessary;
- Put thermostatic control valves on radiators; and
- Install a programmable thermostat for the central heating system.

The constructional elements to enhance your EPC ratings are:

- Install cavity wall insulation if the property has twin skin exterior walls;
- Install solid wall insulation which can be exterior installed or interior fitted;

- Consider upgrading the boiler installation – this can have a significant effect on the EPC rating;
- Check the double glazing – the newer the better, as thermal efficiency has improved significantly in the past 20 years;
- Install immersion heater insulation if not factory installed; and
- Consider renewable energy devices such as solar panels, wind turbines, and ground source heating.

There are currently grants available under the 'Green Home Grants' scheme that will contribute to the required works. I cannot see these grants reducing over time due to the need for the government to be seen to act by the international arena to achieve energy efficiencies. Do your homework on what grants are available to assist you in attaining the appropriate rating.

In 2025 the rules will change. If a property is under rent in 2025, the required EPC E rating will be satisfactory but a C rating will need to be achieved by 2028. If you bring a new property onto the rental market in 2025, it will need a C rating when first advertised.

I would consider planning ahead to work out what needs doing to help you achieve a C rating by 2028 and possibly schedule the works to be done over a period of years to help with budgeting. Of course this is also subject to grants being available.

CERTIFICATIONS SUMMARY

Start with the EPC and the EICR as these may involve further works to bring the property up to the legally required status after the initial inspection.

Organise a gas safety check.

Ensure up-to-date copies of all certificates are given to the tenant on check-in.

NOTES

6

ROOF, CHIMNEY, GUTTERING, AND LOFT

Attention to these areas prior to a new tenancy may alert you to potential damaging leaks which can lead to emergency external roof level works and subsequent internal redecoration. Water damage to the property can go beyond roof level leaks to decoration and floor coverings.

I suggest initial visual checks and then, if necessary, further technical checks and possible repairs before the tenancy or plan them in as the budget allows.

PITCHED ROOF

Check the ridge tiles to see if the pointing and ridge tiles are in good order.

Ensure there are no broken, missing, or badly placed tiles which may allow water ingress during stormy weather.

These areas are easily checked visually, from the ground in most cases.

FLAT ROOF

Ensure there are no leaks to the inside and any chippings are evenly laid. If there are bubbled or cracked areas, consider having these repaired as they may lead to water ingress at some point.

CHIMNEY

Chimneys are sealed to tiles with lead or other flexible flashings. These should be in good order or it is possible for water ingress via the chimney stack to cause damp issues in the rooms below.

If the chimney stack mortar joints appear to be broken or missing, these gaps can allow water ingress.

Check each floor internally where a chimney breast is present, including the loft. Look for water marks on the breast, either at ceiling level or on the face or sides of the breast. Check inside any cupboards that may have been built around the chimney breast for signs of water damage.

Water marks at ceiling level around a chimney breast may indicate an issue with flashing or pointing around the chimney.

Water marks further down a breast could indicate water ingress into the flue from the chimney stack crown, which may be difficult to see from the ground. The crown is built around the chimney pot and is shaped to enable water to run off to the roof tiles. The other cause of this type of damp is poor pointing on the chimney stack itself.

It is definitely worth checking the chimney stack in the loft space, as this is the nearest point to the external chimney structure and can help you work out the source of an issue spotted within the property.

As buildings age, these sorts of issues become more prevalent unless they are monitored and maintained.

If the roof on your rental property is more than 25 years old, it is worth having a roofer carry out an inspection and correct issues such as flashing and tile issues prior to your first tenancy.

Given the risks associated with poorly maintained roofs and chimneys, I would recommend that you consult with a roofer or builder if you suspect issues. Then plan repairs depending upon their urgency. This approach will help you manage the risks and your budget.

GUTTERING

Surprisingly, poorly maintained guttering is a major contributor of water ingress issues through walls, causing damp in rooms below the gutter run. Issues with gutters can sometimes go unnoticed until the damage is seen internally. Gutters that overflow, for whatever reason, and issues with gutter runs that have come adrift from their fixings, may not be immediately obvious.

Water overflow from a gutter can be caused by something as simple as the gutter run being blocked with leaves or debris that has come off the roof area. This debris can block gutters and downpipes during heavy rainfall.

This can consequently lead to damp ingress into the house as water can enter the mortar joints on the walls directly under the gutter run. If damp does ingress through the walls, it may appear as a damp brown patch on the internal face of the affected walls. If damp patches are visible, it is worth checking the guttering for blockages or to see if it has dislodged from its fixing brackets. Also, check the pointing on that elevation as this may have degraded over time, allowing water to ingress more easily.

Sometimes moss can be seen growing out of broken mortar joints. This is a good warning indicator of gutter or downpipe issues. Moss will absorb water and ease the migration of moisture through the wall to the internal face.

Guttering can also develop leak issues at joints or where the gutter joins the downpipe. Downpipes can also have jointing issues or be blocked below the gutter entry point with debris from the roof. This means that joints on the downpipe may leak if the guttering becomes overwhelmed by rain.

The gutter slope (fall) is also important as it ensures that there is a sufficient angle from the gutter start to take water all the way to the nearest downpipe. This will allow the rain to reach the downpipe faster and help prevent overflow if the gutters receive a high volume of water from the roof area during rainfall.

One other area that can contribute to blocked gutters is moss and other debris from the roof area.

In autumn, moss and leaves can accumulate on a pitched tile roof and can be pushed down to the gutter during heavy rain. Add to this that, as a roof ages, mortar and tile debris from ridge and roof tiles can accumulate in the gutter run and you have a recipe for a blockage, especially in downpipes.

I recommend that gutters be cleared at least once every couple of years – every year, if possible, especially where the property is surrounded by trees.

LOFT

Check that the loft insulation is properly laid and that there are no gaps in the corners or at the edges. If there are gaps in the insulation, make sure they are filled in, as this can cause cold spots on the ceiling below and cause condensation damage. Current legislation requires insulation to be 220 – 270 mm thick, dependent upon insulation type used.

If you can see daylight through the roof tiles from within the loft, have the tiles checked externally or reset so that water cannot ingress into the loft.

Lofts are ideal storage areas. They are also areas that may not be built for access due to a lack of suitable flooring. If you have not boarded your loft for safe access and storage it may be worth locking the loft hatch to prevent access by the tenant. Think ahead about the possible risks of access. If in doubt, prevent access during the tenancy.

ROOF, CHIMNEY, GUTTERING, AND LOFT SUMMARY

These areas often don't get the attention they deserve before or during tenancies but they can have a massive cost effect if issues are not tackled as they arise and they then become an urgent incident. Beware, that if any issue has an associated cost that would encourage you to contact your insurer, one of the focus areas from the insurer may be to check if the incident was caused by pre-existing issues that should have been better maintained by the landlord. Failure to maintain can negate cover.

Check the ridge tile line, tiles and chimney structure, and flashing to ensure all are in good order.

Check top floor ceilings and all chimney breasts internally for signs of damp ingress.

Check the guttering and downpipes for any leaks or damage to joints.

Check the guttering for adequate flow from the gutter start point to the downpipe.

Clear or plan in gutter clearance as a regular annual or bi-annual job.

NOTES

7

GARDENS, TREES AND EXTERNAL AREAS

GARDENS

This is an area where tenants can be remiss in their responsibility to carry out the expected upkeep. It is worth ensuring that your expectations are clear, both verbally and in writing.

I recommend that you have the garden made up to the standard that you want it to be kept up to during the tenancy.

Take photos of the current state. This should include the height of bushes, shrubs, and trees.

If any trees and shrubs are growing close to the house and look like they may grow towards windows or guttering, consider having them pruned back. They can cause damage to the property in poor weather and may reduce the amount of light the property receives. It would also be wise to have planned maintenance of trees and shrubs in place to prevent any future potential damage to the property.

Any bushes or shrubs that you expect the tenant to maintain will need to be no higher than 2 metres. This is a generally accepted safe height that a tenant can be expected to reach to carry out any maintenance.

Leylandii is one hedging plant that should be monitored carefully and kept in check as it grows broad and high very quickly and can get out of control. If you have one or more of these plants and the property is to be rented out for a long period of time, consider whether they should be left in place. Individual Leylandii can grow very tall and are treated as trees. At the very least, include these on your planned maintenance list.

Any fences, especially party fences, should be in good condition with no holes – especially if you are marketing the property with pets allowed. If fences are going to need maintenance in the future, include them in your planned maintenance notes.

Paved areas should be free of moss and other growth. If needed, have the area cleaned off, possibly with a jet wash, to prevent a slip risk to the new tenants. They can then be responsible for the ongoing maintenance. Paved areas should be maintained and any height difference of 25 mm between adjacent slabs or flags should be repaired. For your information, the US stipulates 6 mm as the risk threshold. I think their interpretation is more sensible.

TREES

Trees are a magnificent addition to our urban and rural landscapes.

However, these are often in isolation when new tree additions are planned. Little thought goes into the species and planting location. In rental properties, this is just one issue that can affect the tenant-landlord relationship and neighbour relations.

When a house owner lives in a property with trees, they are visible and should action be required, the owner either tackles the pruning themselves or employs a tree surgeon.

However, once that house owner becomes a landlord or an investor buys a property to rent out, trees are usually forgotten in the process. They only come back into frame when an issue arises. Even managing agents don't typically have a proactive tree observation policy which could be valuable in keeping the landlord informed of changes to trees on their property.

Trees quietly grow in the background, and often they outgrow their original planned space with root expansion and overhanging canopies. Trees can affect light into the property, cause damage to roofs and gutters and affect aerial and satellite signals.

They can also cause neighbourly issues and sometimes general aggravation by encroaching on public footpaths and roads.

If a tree's branches or roots are hanging over or burrowing under your neighbour's boundary line, then you have the potential for a dispute on your hands.

Under common law, they have the legal right to prune any branches and roots from your trees that invade their land.

Landlords must be aware of the laws surrounding trees and mindful of the potential disputes and problems concerning trees on their land or neighbouring properties.

If you have trees on your rental property, then be proactive about trimming/pruning. Develop a tree maintenance schedule ahead of the rental.

Employ a tree surgeon to prune the trees back regularly.

Failing that on regular property inspections, get photos of all trees from which you can make decisions on pruning and maintenance.

Use this information to gauge if intervention is required. It will be less costly to have regular pruning than have to deal with the consequences of an overgrown tree causing issues that could have been avoided.

Routine pruning can reduce potential safety issues and the need for costly repairs to buildings or other assets damaged by an overgrown tree or branches that should have been pruned to avoid becoming a liability.

Being proactive can keep management costs low, avoid serious expenses associated with trees over time, and ensure they contribute to a more visually appealing property.

You should ensure that any trees do not interfere and are unlikely to contribute to overhead electricity or telephone cables issues. If they do, the utility companies themselves can trim the trees without reference to you.

Similarly, suppose your trees block access to a public footpath or have dangerous overhanging branches bordering public paths and roads. In that case, you should act swiftly to deal with the issue before the local council intervenes and serves notice requiring appropriate action or takes action and sends you the bill.

In the recent past, a landlord who owned a property that bordered a railway station faced a £5,000 bill for severe pruning back of a tree that had been allowed to grow out of control and during a storm, branches fell off and blew onto the rail line.

Should a tree be identified as dangerous to neighbouring private or public property and people, then it will be worth employing an arborist to check the tree. They can carry out an arboricultural survey that will usually advise a management program to maintain the tree in good health and shape or, if necessary, a plan to have it removed.

As a tree owner, you have a duty of care to others to manage the trees on your rental property and have them professionally inspected and recommended works carried out to keep them in good health.

Trees can be a health and safety issue for your tenants, neighbours and the public. Should an incident happen, you may be liable and not able to call on your insurance policy if it is proven you were negligent.

Should a case be brought against you, how you have approached the management of trees on your property will be considered. Record keeping of tree management activity will be crucial for your defence.

Healthy trees fall over in storms, but if you have not managed the tree and this has been party to the tree failure, this may not help your defence.

Overextended limbs, disease and untreated damage can impact the integrity of a tree, causing it to weaken and increase the probability of failure.

At this point, let me try and explain the difference between an arborist and a tree surgeon.

An arborist is interested in landscaping using trees and devising tree management plans for both planned and existing trees.

They are usually qualified to check the health and safety of trees and, therefore, key to assisting with trees that have developed a disease and advise how the tree should be maintained for the remainder of its life. It will be worth employing an arborist from the get-go should a tree be under suspicion of disease or in danger of causing public harm.

A tree surgeon is more the engineer who manages the pruning and removal of trees. They will call on the services of an arborist to assist with health and safety management in certain circumstances.

In some areas of the UK, certain trees or areas of trees are covered by Tree Preservation Orders (TPO).

The following website will assist you in finding out whether trees on your property are likely or not to be affected should you need to carry out works on them.

https://www.gov.uk/apply-work-on-protected-tree

What is a Tree Preservation Order?

Local councils impose Tree Preservation Orders to protect trees, improving the local environment. You must seek permission to do any work on a tree covered by an order.

A TPO is not restricted to any particular species or size of a tree. You must seek council permission to do any work on a protected tree – even removing a dead branch or pruning a tree causing a nuisance is a grey area.

If consent is refused, you can appeal to have the order overturned.

If the tree is in a Conservation Area, you must give the local council the option to serve a TPO before carrying out any work on the tree. It has six weeks to decide whether to perform a TPO.

Failure to comply with a TPO can result in fines of up to £20,000.

GARDENS, TREES AND EXTERNAL AREAS SUMMARY

Tidy the garden and trim shrubs to a manageable height for the tenant to maintain.

Identify trees and taller shrubs that will be managed by you and ensure these are in a well-maintained condition at the start of the tenancy.

Check paved areas for safety (slip and trip risks).

Provide clear instructions for garden maintenance and include which shrubs the tenant will manage.

Walk the external areas to look for hazards and remove them.

If you have trees on your rental property, develop a tree maintenance schedule ahead of the rental.

Employ a tree surgeon to prune the trees back regularly. Failing that on regular property inspections, get photos of all trees from which you can make decisions on pruning and maintenance.

Act promptly if a tree on your rental property is reported to be causing a public nuisance or affecting utility cables.

If a tree is reported to be in poor health, assess if an arboricultural survey is appropriate to check the health and safety of the tree.

Always check the government website to see if your tree may be in a Conservation Area as your trees may already be under a Tree Protection Order. If so, you must make an application for any works you may want to carry out on the trees.

NOTES

8

GARAGES

The main issue that arises with garages is the door-opening mechanism; ensure it is in good working order. Record the make and model of the door and, if it has an electric drive mechanism, find a technician who is familiar with the brand. This will help reduce call-out costs should the door require repair. If you already work with a technician and you are also working with a managing agent, ensure they have the contractor details. This will prevent unnecessary costs and delays in trying to find a suitable contractor to carry out any repairs. Keep a spare garage key in case the tenant loses the main key.

GARAGES SUMMARY

Check the garage closing mechanisms are in good working condition.

Keep a spare garage door key.

Keep a record of a garage door specialist who has worked on your brand of door.

NOTES

9

BOUNDARIES

First, let me clear up a much-mentioned myth. I have heard many times that a property owner owns the boundary to the right or left of their property. This may be the case but there is no legal basis for this thinking.

The reality is much less clear!

If you are lucky, the boundaries will be marked on the plans held with the property deeds using a T or H to notify the owners. The tail of the T touching any boundary indicates the owner of that property is responsible for the upkeep of the boundary. If there is an H, basically two T's with the tails touching, then this indicates a party boundary for which both property owners are liable. If this information is not present on the title plans, neighbourly discussion may be the only way forward. If discussion leads nowhere and boundary repairs are still required, then you can turn to the courts or reach out to The Royal Institution of Chartered Surveyors. They run a mediation service that can assist with boundary disputes.

Why have I mentioned this? As a landlord you may not be aware of the boundary ownership around your property. Now, imagine you are remote from the property – possibly add a managing agent into the mix – and an incident happens regarding a boundary, such as a damaged fence, wall, or hedging. How do you manage to work out a way forward?

One way is to have conversations with the neighbours before you rent the property out. Make a record of the agreed boundary responsibilities along with neighbours' contact details and keep them safe in case you need them. The amount of time lost when a boundary failure such as a storm-damaged fence occurs can be excessive if you are trying to find out who is responsible. Often, managing agents face reticence from the tenant to approach the next-door neighbour to obtain contact details and letters to the neighbour are often ignored.

BOUNDARIES SUMMARY

Check that fences are in good condition and, if possible, identify ownership.

Know your boundary ownership responsibilities. Check your deed plans and record your neighbour's contact details in case a boundary incident occurs.

NOTES

10

WINDOWS AND DOORS

These can be areas where urgent issues can creep up and weather changes can lead to complaints from tenants about the effectiveness of windows or doors.

Take time to check that the windows and doors in your rental property are in good working order.

Decide if any repairs are needed and if they need to be completed prior to the start of the tenancy or if they can be scheduled during the tenancy to help cash flow.

WINDOWS

All windows should effectively seal and lock to keep out the weather. They should open and close easily. Windows are an area of potential complaints, mainly due to draughts, water ingress due to damaged seals, or window mechanisms that don't lock the window into the frame sufficiently allowing draughts in.

If the windows let in draughts, it could be that the seals have perished in places or the opening and closing mechanisms are damaged and need repair or replacement.

If you notice potential issues with windows. consider having them repaired prior to the start of the tenancy or plan the works during the tenancy and before autumn/winter. This will help prevent them from becoming an urgent issue.

For UPVC windows try to use a contractor who is familiar with UPVC window repairs as the mechanisms can be very different to their timber counterparts.

Timber windows, especially sash windows, should be repaired by timber window specialists. They will have more knowledge on sourcing weights and other parts for sash windows.

If windows require keys to operate the locks you should have at least two copies, one set for you and/or the managing agent and one set for the tenant. Make a list of which window locks have associated keys and ensure the tenant has checked and signed this list to confirm each lockable window has an associated key. This checked list should be added to the inventory.

It is not uncommon for tenants to lose the odd key or sometimes the entire bunch, hence my recommendation to get duplicates.

If you have supplied the tenant with an agreed set of window keys and they lose them, then you should be ready to charge for the replacement set. If you do not have a spare set you may need to consider changing window handles at £50 to £100 per window. If you have a duplicate set, you can charge for an individual key copy or for a full replacement set of keys.

There are eBay sellers in the UK who will supply spares at reasonable costs – just key in 'UPVC keys'.

DOORS

Internal doors

Internal timber doors are usually full timber panels or part glazed.

All internal doors should be checked prior to rental to ensure they comply with safety regulations and to ensure they do not have any defects that could become repair issues later.

Hinges can become loose in the frame if they have not been properly secured, possibly by smaller than optimal screws being used or the door may have been rehung without the holes being filled.

The latch, handle, or strike plate in the door frame can become worn. This can lead to either the latch becoming jammed into the frame or the latch not remaining in the keep when the door is closed allowing the door to slip open.

These issues can be tackled by a handyman. If you believe there may be issues with any of the internal doors, these are worth checking before the tenancy as door issues can crop up and can cause unnecessary repeat visits during the tenancy.

If a tenant becomes stuck in a room due to a faulty latch, there is a possibility that this could escalate to an emergency call-out, incurring extra cost.

Internal doors with glass that extend down to a height of less than 80 cm from the floor must have safety glass installed.

One potentially costly issue to bear in mind is that if you have matching handles throughout the house, if one door has to have the handles changed it may not be possible to match the existing ones.

External doors

Exterior doors can develop several types of issues depending on whether they are UPVC or timber doors.

▶ UPVC doors

The most prevalent issues I have encountered with UPVC doors are related to handles and mechanisms. After a lot of use the handles become loose and then stop working, with the locking mechanism effectively causing closing and locking issues. The door mechanisms can become faulty and the moving parts on the door are not able to interlock with the corresponding slots in the frame mechanism.

In addition to the above issues, hinges can become misaligned and cause the door to be difficult to close and open.

Door seals can then be damaged if the door has become misaligned. Seals also perish naturally over time.

If you experience issues with a UPVC door closing or locking or there are draughts between the door and frame, it may be wise to have this checked out prior to rental. The cost of having these type of repairs undertaken prior to rental will almost definitely be less costly than an emergency call-out during the tenancy. This could prevent you from being faced with a future bill for an out-of-hours call when the tenant can't unlock or lock the house door. The costs for an out-of-hours temporary fix followed by a permanent repair can be as much as £300.

Tenants are becoming more aware of security and safety issues and if locks appear to cause either potential security or safety issues it is possible they may come up in discussion during the tenancy if not during pre-tenancy negotiations.

▶ Timber doors

Timber doors have simpler locking mechanisms than UPVC doors and these can mean repairs are less costly.

The main issues are similar to UPVC doors: hinges, locking mechanisms, handles, and doors allowing draughts.

Hinges can become loose causing the door to be difficult to open and close. This may mean the hinges need to be fixed or replaced.

If a door is sticking or binding on the top or bottom, the probable cause is damp swelling the timber. This will be an ongoing issue either permanently or during winter, possibly becoming less critical during warmer months.

If the door is sticking between the door edge and the frame, this can be due to the door having been over-painted to the extent that there is not a sufficient gap between the door and the frame.

I would recommend external timber doors are painted or varnished every 3 to 5 years with good quality materials. This will help maintain the integrity of the door and prevent weathering from becoming an issue.

Locks and keys can become worn. Check the keys work in the door lock without effort. If you find a problem, it could be either the key or the lock mechanism. Resolve this before the rental to reduce the risk of emergency call-outs during the tenancy.

Always have at least two spare keys. You will need one and if you are working with a management agent they will need one too.

If your tenant changes the locks, for whatever reason, they should provide the same number of keys you had for the original lock to you or the managing agent. If they refuse, you are entitled to change the lock again so that you have keys that will enable you to access the property within the permitted access notice period. In the first instance, tenants are meant to ask for permission to change the locks.

▶ Flat doors

External flat and apartment doors have become a emotive topic since the Grenfell Tower incident.

Main flat doors will need to meet certain regulations and be fit to protect both the householder and other residents in the block in the event of an emergency. Block management companies should advise on what is required as they are legally responsible for carrying out an appropriate building fire risk assessment.

The lease terms and conditions will determine the person responsible for changes to, or replacement of, a flat or apartment door. In some leases the building owner is responsible and in others the leaseholder is responsible. If the building owner is responsible and works are required to your property door, they will usually reflect this in the service charge.

If you as the leaseholder are responsible for the main door, then you will probably need to submit your planned changes to the building management company and apply for Building Regulations approval from the local council due to the fire risk implications. Generally, flat doors should be fire-rated for 30 minutes and be self-closing.

There are currently no regulations that cover lock types for flat doors, but it is a generally accepted good practice to have key access externally and a thumb turn type lock internally to speed up emergency egress.

WINDOWS AND DOORS SUMMARY

Check for draughty windows and possible faulty opening and locking mechanisms and repair (or plan to) before the next winter period.

Record which windows have keys. Review this with the tenant. Add a detailed list and photo of keys to the inventory.

Check that internal timber doors with glass meet the regulations.

Check internal doors for correct operation: hinges, handles keeps and latches.

Check external doors to ensure the closing and locking mechanisms work effectively with no effort required.

Check all door seals are in good order and the doors do not allow in draughts.

Consider main door locks – if they are key-based externally and internally, consider changing to a thumb turn internally, if technically possible. This should be strongly considered if you are renting a flat. There are no regulations but, given the Grenfell incident, this would be a sensible and appropriate move.

Flat doors – work with your building management team to ensure your flat entrance door meets the current standards.

NOTES

11

LOCKS AND KEYS

This is an area that often gets overlooked before a tenancy starts and attention really should be paid to prevent you as a landlord being blamed for having sub-standard locks in incidents such as break-ins.

Check the locks on external doors before you let the property.

Should the tenant opt for household insurance, their insurer will want details on what lock types are currently in place.

Ensure all external door locks meet the minimum standards to enable tenants to get contents insurance and also to provide the tenant with adequate security. To check the lock build standard, look at the face of the lock in the edge of the door. It should have a kite mark and the relevant BS standard engraved on it.

If the doors are timber and your budget allows, try to ensure they are 5-lever locks manufactured to British Standard BS3621. This is now the de facto standard for basic timber door security. These can be purchased in mortice lock, sash lock, or night latch style. As discussed in the Doors and Windows section, I would always recommend a night latch on the interior for fast egress in the event of an emergency.

If the doors are UPVC or composite, then a euro cylinder SS312 Diamond euro lock is one of the lock types recommended. This will have a diamond with 3 stars engraved on the lock face.

Who should have key copies? You as the landlord, a set for the tenant, and one for the managing agent if you have employed one. Normally each registered tenant should be given a set of keys. I refer to set as one for the main door and one for the rear or side door.

What if the tenant changes the locks mid-tenancy? Ensure there is a clause in the tenancy agreement advising that the tenant must request permission and provide duplicate sets to you and the managing agent (if there is one) as soon as the locks have been changed.

At the end of the tenancy you should decide if you want to change the locks for the next tenant. Why? There are a few reasons you may want to change the locks when one tenant leaves. Perhaps the tenancy relationship did not go well or there were many contractors who had keys to enter the property.

Most burglaries in the UK are via non-forced entry through open access points or acquired keys.

LOCKS AND KEYS SUMMARY

Head off complaints about lock specifications from tenants. Make sure the locks comply with the relevant standards for the door type.

Ensure enough key sets are available for all relevant parties.

NOTES

12

DECORATION

In general, in a rental property, wall and ceiling decoration is best kept as neutral as possible and ensure a matt finish for ceilings and a silk finish for walls to enable easy cleaning of scuffs and marks by the tenant or in between tenancies.

Use white or magnolia emulsions on ceilings and walls. Use gloss, satin, or possibly eggshell on door frames, skirting boards, and any other woodwork. All of these paint types can be easily cleaned during and between tenancies.

If patterned wallpaper exists on walls, bear in mind that if it becomes damaged you will need to be able to patch it, replace the paper, or remove the wallpaper and paint the wall.

BATHROOMS

If possible, paint the walls and ceilings with an anti-mould emulsion bathroom paint. This will help deter mould growth. Condensation that can cause mould growth is discussed later in more detail.

Ensure wall tiles and grouting are in good condition. This will prevent water penetrating the tile joints into the wall, causing the tiles to loosen, or damp appearing on a party wall or leaking into the floor below.

If the flooring is tiled, make sure the grouting is in good condition and, if not, have it repaired. Tenants can complain on the basis of safety if the grout is coming out as it could cause injury, especially if there are children in the property. Missing grout on a tiled floor can also cause water egress to lower floors, causing damage to ceilings and walls.

If the flooring is sheet vinyl or another laminate style, ensure there are no issues with the material that could be considered a trip hazard. If the flooring is peeling at joints or edges, reseal it to the subfloor.

Ventilation is another possible problem area in both bathrooms and kitchens.

A lack of ventilation can cause condensation to build up from hot water used for baths and showers and lead to condensation damp and mould damage to walls and ceilings.

I strongly urge you to consider either a humidity-controlled fan or one that can operate in league with the bathroom light switch or have a motion-sensor PIR system. PIR and humidity-controlled fans can be especially helpful when the room is used during daylight hours. Humidity-controlled models turn on when the humidity level (amount of moisture in the air) reaches a pre-set level and then turns off when the level drops back to another pre-set level.

Installing a fan like this is an insurance policy in case tenants do not use windows as often as they should to control the moisture build-up, not only in the bathroom but also in the house in general.

KITCHEN

As with the bathroom, paint all walls and ceiling with anti-mould paint if possible, as steam from cooking and washing up can be a major cause of condensation.

If there is a cooker or hob hood installed, ensure the filter is replaced and that the fan works effectively. A common householder misconception is that a hood is ducted to the outside. Obviously, some are but the majority only have filters to absorb grease, smoke, and odours.

It may be worthwhile to install a humidity-controlled fan to reduce the presence and effects of condensation during cooking and washing up, as in the bathroom.

If there is no fan in the kitchen, consider an instruction set to advise tenants to open a window when cooking to avoid moisture accumulating in the house and to close internal doors into other rooms from the kitchen. The instruction set can be handed to the tenant on check-in.

FAN MAINTENANCE

Advise tenants that they must keep extractor fans clean and clear of dust and grease. If a call-out is requested for an extractor fan and it is found that it is not working due to an accumulation of dust or grease, they should be liable for cost of the call-out.

BEDROOMS AND LIVING AREAS

These should be painted in neutral silk paints on walls and matt on the ceilings. This will make it easier to touch up, if required.

DECORATING MATERIALS

If you have any paints left over from any redecoration, label them with the locations used and store them in a cool place at the rental property to prolong the paint life. It may be worth having these listed on the inventory so they are not mistakenly thrown out. This means they will be available to the tenants in case touch-ups are required during the tenancy, for contractors carrying out maintenance, or to enable the tenant at end of the tenancy to leave the house in the same state as when they checked in.

If possible, keep records of the brands and paint types used in each room for future reference, in case you want to paint a small area or touch up in between tenancies and where you don't have any leftover paints from the original decoration. This could save you the cost of a decorator or your time repainting entire rooms.

DECORATION SUMMARY

Use matt emulsion on ceilings and washable silk paints on walls. On timber use gloss, satin, or eggshell for longevity and ease of cleaning.

In bathrooms and kitchens use washable silk with an anti-mould additive.

Check the condition of the grouting for tiles on walls and flooring.

Check the bathroom and kitchen for adequate ventilation either with an easily openable window or with a working extractor fan. In the absence of active fans in these rooms consider an instruction set for the tenants on how to ventilate the rooms and how to avoid condensation build-up.

Leave any residual paints at the property so the tenant can touch up where necessary.

NOTES

13

ELECTRICAL

This is another area that may escape focus pre-tenancy unless there are pre-existing repair issues.

There are new regulations that require a 5-year electrical integrity check in rental properties. There will be more on this in the Certification section.

After check-in, tenants often discover switches for which there is no apparent use and want to know their function. Sometimes switches for certain functions can't be found, for instance, external lights.

From a householder perspective, a thorough check of the property electrical system, by you or a third party, will be valuable to resolve issues or to make note of items such as redundant switches as well as the location of switches for appliances and external lights.

CONSUMER UNIT

The tenant should be advised of the consumer unit location. All circuit breakers should be appropriately labelled with what they control (e.g., downstairs sockets or upstairs lighting).

This will make it easier for you, the tenant, or a managing agent's maintenance personnel to try and resolve a problem without having to call an electrician. It will also be easier to identify the likely underlying cause of an electrical issue.

A sizable number of electrical issues can usually be sourced to failed appliances, some of which may not have been supplied with the tenancy. An appliance check approach may save you an electrician call-out. Tenants can be resistant to going through an appliance check analysis to find out what the issue is but it is very valuable as it may prevent an electrician call-out.

SWITCHES AND SOCKETS

Ensure all switches and sockets are working or identified as not working. A small Dymo label advising 'no function' will be helpful and probably eliminate irritating phone calls about the function of a switch. If there are any faulty sockets that would be considered part of the normal sockets available it may be worthwhile to have them repaired or replaced. A failed socket could lead to the tenant plugging too many items into another socket or an extension cable which may present a fire risk.

Hidden socket locations for appliances should be recorded for items like ovens, fridge freezers, washing machines, etc., and this will help to reduce time to resolve issues by enabling appliances to be isolated faster.

Switches for boilers, immersion heaters, external lights, etc., should be labelled in case of maintenance issues to assist in a phone-based analysis and to provide the tenant with information about which switches control the various appliances and systems in the house.

LIGHT FITTINGS, BULBS, AND SMOKE DETECTOR BATTERIES

Ensure all light fittings are functioning and that the bulbs or lights in them are working at the start of the tenancy. Once the tenant moves in, they will be responsible for changing the bulbs but not the fittings.

PAT TESTING FOR PORTABLE ELECTRICAL APPLIANCES

It is not a legal requirement to have any portable appliances tested (e.g., toasters, kettles) but if you do provide any portable electrical appliances, it is best to have these tested every 1 or 2 years. This is to ensure that if an incident occurs where an appliance is involved in a safety-related incident, you will have a proven record of due diligence if a legal case is brought against you.

ELECTRICAL SUMMARY

List the location of the consumer unit in the inventory.

Label the circuit breakers in case a phone-based analysis of electrical issues becomes necessary.

Ensure all switches and sockets work or are labelled otherwise.

Check that all light fittings are in working order and that all lights are working.

If you provide any portable appliances in the rental, consider having them PAT tested and plan periodic PAT tests.

NOTES

14

SMOKE, HEAT, AND CARBON MONOXIDE DETECTORS

The regulations in all countries, including England, Scotland, Northern Ireland, and Wales, have been changing at different rates over the past few years and different rules currently operate in all countries.

It can be confusing, so below I have listed the rules as they currently stand for each country and have then made a recommendation based on best practice that will help landlords UK-wide to provide the best safety measures for their tenants and reduce landlord risks related to fire and carbon monoxide issues.

ENGLAND

In domestic rental properties in England, a smoke detector is required on each floor of the property.

These are ideally placed at the base of the stairs to cover the ground floor and on the landing area of each floor where there is living accommodation.

No heat detector is currently required for a kitchen or any other room.

Carbon monoxide detectors must be fitted in any property room where an appliance burning gas, oil, or solid fuel is located. The regulations exclude gas cookers, gas hobs or gas ovens. No carbon monoxide detector is currently required for oil boiler installations.

All detectors can be battery or mains powered.

The tenant is responsible for checking the detectors, currently recommended monthly.

The landlord is responsible for repairing or replacing any detector where it is found to be faulty by the tenant or on a property inspection.

Once advised, failure to repair or replace a faulty alarm can lead to a £5000 issued by the local authority should the repair or replacement not be undertaken within reasonable timescales.

The landlord is expected to check all detectors at the tenancy start and record this event. The best place to record it is on the inventory.

If the landlord is having difficulty gaining access to install, replace or repair any detectors, demonstrating these access attempts will mean keeping copies of letters, emails or texts and possibly a summary of the dated attempts

SCOTLAND

One smoke detector is required for each floor in a hallway or on a landing, plus one in what is considered the main living space.

These must be interlinked.

A heat detector is required in the kitchen interlinked to the smoke detectors.

Carbon monoxide detectors are required in any room with oil, gas, or solid fuel appliance. Cooking appliances are excluded.

Detectors can be mains or battery operated but must have sealed batteries to prevent tampering and any requirement to change batteries during the detector's life.

There are no requirements for either smoke, heat or carbon monoxide alarms to be mains powered.

NORTHERN IRELAND

The new Private Tenancies Act 2022 stipulates that *sufficient* smoke detection and carbon monoxide detection appliances are present to warn occupants of the risks.

Tenants are responsible for taking proper care of the detectors.

The legislation leaves a lot of discretion to landlords and their advisors. I think this is not prescriptive enough and could lead to poor implementation of detectors to provide adequate safety.

WALES

All Properties must have mains-powered interlinked smoke detectors on each floor. Any additional smoke detectors fitted as optional may be battery powered.

A heat detector for a kitchen is not mandatory.

Carbon monoxide detectors must be fitted in any room where an appliance burning gas, oil, or solid fuel is located. This includes gas cookers, gas hobs or gas ovens. These detectors can be battery-powered.

All detectors must be tested on tenant check-in, and if a battery or the unit fails, the landlord must replace the battery or repair the detector.

BEST PRACTICE THOUGHTS

So, the regulations vary between the four countries of the UK. I have to say, it would seem far more logical to have a joined-up approach to household fire safety, given the risks of fire and carbon monoxide can affect more than one household in any one incident.

I would suggest that a sensible approach for any landlord is to follow a best practice approach which I have taken from our four home nations, should the budget allow:

- Install a smoke detector on every floor with living accommodation
- Add a smoke detector in any main living space, such as a living room or a living/dining room
- Install a heat detector in the kitchen
- Where possible, install mains-operated interlinked versions or sealed lithium battery-operated and interlinked (except in Wales, where they must be mains-operated).
- Install carbon monoxide detectors in any room with a gas, oil, or solid-fuel appliance (except

for gas cookers - apart from Wales, where a carbon monoxide detector is required for cooking appliances).

- If opting for battery operated - use only sealed type and remove removal battery models to remove the risk of the tenant not changing the battery as required.

In 2019, more than 50 people died of carbon monoxide poisoning in England and Wales alone. One death is too many when carbon monoxide detectors are so cheap to install.

Smoke, carbon monoxide, and heat detector models from various manufacturers can be interlinked, making the warning system really robust. If a linked carbon monoxide detector goes off, even if you are remote from the issue, the heat, smoke or carbon monoxide detector closest to you will warn you of the danger.

If an unfortunate incident does occur, this approach will demonstrate that you took the safety of your tenants seriously.

Ensure the detectors are tested on check-in and any property inspections and the results are recorded on the inventory and inspection reports. Make sure the tenants are educated on how to test the detectors and how frequently:

Tenants should check the detectors monthly. Record this process on an addendum to the tenancy agreement.

Where battery-operated smoke detectors are permissible, I advise choosing sealed lithium battery versions with a lifetime warranty and an end-of-life date printed on the detector. Record this date to know when it is due to be changed. Older detector versions have 9-volt batteries, which are expensive. Battery-operated lithium detectors are relatively cheap; I would opt for these. It takes out the need for the tenant to change the battery.

Your responsibility is to ensure whatever detectors are installed are working at the beginning of the tenancy and replacing them when they become faulty or reach the end of life. During the tenancy, the tenant must ensure they are working, change batteries when necessary (for battery-operated versions), and advise the landlord or managing agent if the detector is out of date or stops working. You should replace the non-working detector as soon as is practical.

Smoke detectors should not be substituted for heat detectors. If smoke detectors are used in a kitchen area, they may erroneously be set off by exposure to smoke and steam, causing unnecessary distress. Heat detectors are activated by an increase in temperature, such as from a fire on the hob. If linked to the integrated smoke detector system, all detectors will go off simultaneously, giving tenants a chance to egress from other areas in the property before the effects of the emergency reach their location.

Where heat detectors are optional, they should be considered an additional measure and a more effective method to detect a fire in the kitchen; for instance, the kitchen door may be closed to other parts of the property, and therefore, if interlinked, they can act as an early warning of danger to enable safe egress from the property.

SMOKE, HEAT, AND CARBON MONOXIDE DETECTORS SUMMARY

The regulations differ across the U.K. Ensure you meet the minimum standards required by law in your country.

Do not under spec what you install. Use sealed lithium battery versions where permitted to reduce management requirements by tenants.

Carry out pre-tenancy checks on all detectors and record end-of-life dates of long-life detectors to ensure you change them before that date.

NOTES

15

APPLIANCES

Including white goods in a home rental can increase the number of interested prospects as most tenants will not want the extra expense of purchasing their own.

The critical white goods required and expected for a tenancy are a cooker or hob and oven. Anything else is considered optional, fridge, freezer, washing machine, dryer and dishwasher.

If white goods are included as part of your rental, you need to be clear who is responsible for maintenance from the start. Section 11 of The Landlord and Tenant Act 1985 allows landlords to move responsibility for maintenance to the tenant should it be something considered appropriate.

In most tenancy agreements, the landlord is responsible for maintaining white goods.

Some landlords gift white goods, especially if the appliances are ageing, with a note in the tenancy agreement that the tenant repairs or replaces appliances during the tenancy. If an item is gifted, do not include it in the inventory.

If the tenant replaces a gifted appliance during the tenancy, they will own it and probably take the replacement with them at check-out.

So, if you think any other appliances carry a possible risk of needing repairs in the short term, either replace them with new ones or negotiate them out of the agreement by gifting them.

It is usual for landlords who move out of a house to rent it out, to leave the appliances in place.

If you provide white goods and want to pass the maintenance liability to the tenant, you could soften the deal by providing extended warranties. You could then provide the warranty details to the tenant. The management of the appliances would then be in their hands as the householder. Your administration would include changing the authorised contacts as tenants change over time.

Even if you work through a managing agent and have extended warranties, I would suggest you hand the maintenance of white goods to the tenant to ensure there is no confusion where the tenant may think you are responsible because the managing agent is handling the maintenance management.

I think two areas to keep in mind if you pass white goods maintenance to the tenant.

If a manufacturer recall occurs, then you should handle the process.

Consider replacing an appliance if it fails after the end of the extended warranty (suggest 5- 7 years - the average practical working life of an appliance).

A postscript to the above is that several companies offer extended white goods; google them and ask your insurance provider.

Register white goods with the manufacturers or their nominated agents. If an agent manages your property, ensure they know about these warranties. For any appliance already installed that is currently under warranty, keep that information safe as well. The amount of time wasted trying to find this information in the event of an emergency or urgent repair is not to be underestimated, especially if you are working with a managing agent.

If you supply appliances such as a washing machine, dryer, fridge, or fridge freezer, ensure you have all the product information available if you or the managing agent needs to appoint a repair contractor.

I recommend that you only leave copies of product information and appliance instruction sets at the rental property. Either provide photocopies or take photos of the documents and compile them into a pdf file or include links to valuable sites such as manufacturer product sites. Provide a data key to the tenant with all the information they need and have a photo of the data key in the inventory. Alternatively, you can share a google document, which could be updated with any new appliance information over time.

Just a quick note on appliance instruction sets. Do not underestimate the value of making these available to the tenant. The tenant is the householder and should realise they have responsibilities for user maintenance of appliances. Tenant responsibility should be pointed out at the start of the tenancy and enforced if problems occur where the tenant is considered liable to rectify the issue. As an illustration, dishwashers can become blocked up with food debris in the drain and the spray arms. Who do you think should be responsible for unblocking them during the tenancy? You would be surprised how many tenants think the landlord should handle it. Some tenants feel that anything other than emptying the drain filter should fall to the landlord. Just because removing the spray arms and cleaning them out to remove food debris is slightly more in-depth than pulling a filter out and swishing it under a tap, tenants often believe this is not a task they should undertake!

If a cleaning or other recommended processes are in an instruction set as a user maintenance process, it is the tenant's responsibility. If the tenant wants a contractor to carry out the work, they should pay.

If an appliance needs replacing during the tenancy, make sure you are clear with your contractor about the replacement specification and your budget. However, be careful to replace with a similar specification at least. Otherwise, you may encounter a complaint from the tenant. Often a contractor will offer a trade-pack version from a merchant; not always an efficient long-term solution. Usually, based on price, these tend to be lower quality, aimed at contractors winning business with landlords.

If an appliance is renewed, register the warranty as part of the works agreed with your contractor.

Warranties are an excellent cost saver, but you must provide a certain level of service delivery to your tenant as a landlord. If a hob breaks down and the manufacturer's service agent cannot attend for seven days, this would probably be considered unacceptable in letting terms as preparing hot meals is viewed as a tenant's right. In this case, you may need to revert to a local contractor to repair and lose the warranty benefit on this occasion.

I strongly advise against supplying any portable appliances such as kettles, coffee makers, irons, toasters, microwaves, and even standalone electric heaters, unless they form a part of the entire heating system.

The reason for not supplying these is the management time and cost to resolve repair issues with these appliances.

A general rule of thumb is if it is light enough to lift and plugs into a socket, do not provide them in the tenancy.

The additional consideration of PAT testing (portable appliance testing) is discussed in the Electrical section and should be considered due to potential liability if an accident were to occur.

An account needs to be taken of your rental profile, and possibly, in some higher-end rentals, it may be more pertinent to supply these portable items. If this is the case, plan PAT testing either annually or bi-annually. If the appliances are being installed as new, then take advantage of any manufacturer warranties.

WASHING MACHINES AND DRYERS

If you are supplying a washing machine already installed in the property, clean it thoroughly using recommended cleaning products and ensure the filter is clear and the seal and drum are thoroughly clean.

Washing machines need user maintenance. As with my illustration above, tenants often do not know about the existence of a filter. The tenant should be advised on how to clean the filter. If an appliance engineer is engaged at any point and reports back on the cause as a blocked filter you should consider charging the tenant. If this routine task has been made clear at the start of the tenancy, there should be no reason that you should pay.

Washing machines can start to smell after a number of low-temperature washes. This can lead to mould growth both on the drum and on the door seal, which will cause odours. Unless action is taken to remove the mould it will continue to grow, causing further blackening of areas such as the door seal and the internal drum areas, which is not always visible. It then becomes increasingly difficult to remove the mould. Clearance of this problem should be down to the tenant using one of many well-published methods available on the internet. The tenant should be advised at the start of the tenancy about periodic cleaning of the machine.

If you intend to supply a washer dryer or ducted dryer, ensure this is in good order and ducted through an external wall at the start of the tenancy. Condensation mould on walls and the ceiling can result if the hose is allowed to vent inside the house. Where a vent hose has not been ducted externally it is not unknown for tenants to vent it into the room space rather than through a nearby door.

Condensing dryers are an option and are available in two types: plumbed to a waste outlet or with a reservoir that collects the water and needs to be emptied periodically. If you supply a reservoir model, ensure the tenant is aware of the need to empty it.

FRIDGES AND FRIDGE FREEZERS

Check existing fridges and freezer units to ensure they are in good working order. The door seals should be in good condition. Doors should open and close easily. Fridges should not have any ice or moisture build-up.

Ensure you have defrosted the freezer and cleaned it out.

Fridges and freezers are areas often neglected by tenants.

If a fridge is not cleaned regularly, dirt build-up can lead to the rear drain hole becoming blocked. This hole is meant to allow excess moisture build-up to reach a reservoir in the base of the fridge where it evaporates. If this hole is blocked, moisture will build up on shelves and possibly ice up on the rear wall of the fridge. This vent hole can be cleared with a cotton bud or turkey baster full of warm water being inserted to push the dirt down the tube into the reservoir.

If, on inspection, it is noticed that there is ice build-up in the freezer, ask the tenant to defrost it as this can lead to a loss of performance. It can also cause issues such as the freezer door not closing properly leading to door seal damage and further ice build-up.

If the freezer is not a frost-free version it will need to be defrosted from time to time in any case.

DISHWASHERS

Dishwashers should be cleaned before the start of the tenancy. The main areas are the filter in the base of the machine and the spray arms which get a build-up of food debris over time.

The manufacturer's instruction set should advise on how to clean these.

Tenants should use proprietary cleaners regularly to keep the dishwasher clean and be advised to do this if they smell odours coming from the appliance. This is a common issue reported by tenants.

COOKING APPLIANCES

Cooking appliances such as a gas or electric hob plus oven or a standalone cooker are expected to be installed in most tenancies.

Where possible try to supply an electric oven.

Electric ovens have more effective heat output control and therefore householders enjoy an easier time using them as opposed to gas versions which are considered 'old hat'.

One area that can cause an issue is oven timers. I recommend that you ensure the tenant has the instruction set to manage the oven, including the timer. I know of a number of instances where timers have locked the oven in a mode where the oven appears not to be working.

Modern hobs fitted into the work surface rarely have the make and model on the top surface and when issues arise with them the only way to obtain this information is by accessing the area underneath the hob. This can be a major operation, especially if the hob has been sealed in using mastics. If you install a new hob, record these details in case of repairs.

The only other method is to try and match the product online. Take a photo of the hob unit to help match it against an online photo. Be aware that this approach can sometimes give you the incorrect match for spare parts.

I have seen a number of incidents where spare parts cannot be sourced due to difficulties with matching the installed version and it has been cheaper for landlords to install a new hob.

If there is a hob already in place, record the measurements in case a replacement is required in the future.

MICROWAVE

There is no requirement to supply a microwave but, if you decide to include one in the tenancy and you are buying new, try to choose one with simple operation.

If the property already has an integrated version, record the make, model, and size to assist with any necessary replacement process.

Finding replacement integrated microwaves that fit the space can be time-consuming.

Integrated versions tend to be twice the price of the equivalent freestanding model.

APPLIANCE COVER OPTIONS

Consider appliance cover from a company such as British Gas, HomeServe, Domestic and General or Zest.

They offer comprehensive cover and are an easy place to start if you have little time. Bear in mind when buying this type of policy to check their service delivery standards.

For instance, if the cooker or hob stops working and they can only visit 7 days later, you as a landlord may need to act more rapidly to ensure you meet the requirements of the tenancy agreement. It is generally accepted in the UK that heating, cooking, and hot water are seen as critical resources and only limited down-time is acceptable to meet your responsibilities under the tenancy agreement. This can vary but anything beyond 48 hours will probably not be acceptable, and you may be expected to supply temporary replacement facilities and even financial recompense from when the issue first occurred.

When you look into appliance cover ask about the service delivery agreement to ensure you will be able to meet your obligations if you subscribe to a policy.

If you have an appliance policy, consider the following to help you manage the repairs effectively.

If there is no excess payable on the policy then, as each claim arises, allow the tenant to report the issue to the policy provider directly. This will help make reports of the issues and appointments much easier.

To enable this, the tenant details should be passed to the policy provider as account nominees to prevent refusal when they call the policy helpline and to help avoid potential call-out delays. You will also need to provide the tenants with the contact details for the provider and any policy or security details to assist them.

Going forward, any new tenant details should be passed to the policy provider.

This is worth mentioning as this is often forgotten and causes delays to repairs and unnecessary alternative contractor call-outs, which may result in losing the warranty benefit.

APPLIANCES SUMMARY

Ensure all appliance information is recorded in case of breakdown, including make, model, and serial number, as well as any warranty information. If you are working with a managing agent, pass this information to them.

Consider if you need to include certain appliances. Can the supply of appliances such as a dryer or dishwasher be used as a basis for rent negotiation?

Ensure a clear list of appliances to be managed by you are listed on the inventory, and any that are gifted are listed in the Tenancy Agreement addendum.

Leave instruction set copies for each appliance at the property in hard copy or on a data key.

Consider compiling a tenancy household care summary that can be added to the tenancy agreement addendum that advises the tenant of their responsibilities to maintain the appliances. If a technical issue arises due to failure to carry out householder duties, they may bear the cost.

Remember Section 11 of The Landlord and Tenant Act 1985 allows you to hand over maintenance management of white goods to the tenant. Consider this as an option and also consider an extended warranty policy in tandem. Extended warranties will help sell the idea to the tenant and reduce your management time on any issues that arise.

Even if the appliance maintenance is to lie with the tenant - ensure they are all on the inventory - because they are yours. Also, the Tenancy Agreement needs to stipulate the maintenance responsibility conditions

Consider appliance cover from a company such as British Gas, HomeServe, Domestic and General and Zest. They offer comprehensive cover and are easy to set up if you have little time. When buying this type of policy, bear in mind to check their service delivery practices.

NOTES

16

UTILITIES

At check-in, take meter readings for the gas, water, and electricity, and ask the tenant to check and confirm them once they have moved in to avoid any dispute later on. If you are working with a managing agent, then ask them to record the check-in meter reads on the inventory. Ensure you pay off any balances due to your utility providers so you are not pursued after the rental has begun and give them your home address so any bills do not go to the rental property.

ELECTRICITY

If there is no smart meter in the property it may be pertinent to have one installed where you want it rather than have the tenant decide on the location. The current regulations allow for every home to have a smart meter whether they are owner-occupied or tenanted. Tenants tend to be quite energy conscious so it is probable that you will receive a request to authorise a smart meter installation at some point. There was a plan for all providers to have offered domestic customers a smart meter by the end of 2021. This has been extended as take-up was less than expected.

WATER

There will probably be a stop tap (stop cock) in the pavement for the property but there may not be one within the property where the water supply can be isolated with ease. If this is the case it will be a good idea to have one installed as close to where the mains water supply enters the property. Having a stop tap installed internally can prevent major damage if a leak develops. Tenants or contractors then have easy access to switch off the supply should an incident occur. I have seen extensive and unnecessary property damage where it was not possible for the tenant to switch off the water supply after discovering a leak and they had to wait for a plumber to arrive.

Most stop taps are sited under the kitchen sink as this is usually the first point where mains water joins the internal plumbing system. Other locations can be the garage, utility room, cellar, under the stairs, or in a ground-floor toilet or bathroom.

I cannot recommend strongly enough that the location of the internal stop tap be recorded so the tenant knows where it is in the case of an emergency. This is best placed on the inventory as the location can be recorded with a photo. Ensure your tenant knows the location of the stop tap and the water meter. It may also be worth tagging the stop tap with a label.

GAS

If there is gas in the property, ensure the location of the gas meter is known to the tenant and, as with the water stop tap, this is best done on the inventory.

The gas meter has an isolation valve on the inbound mains gas pipe. This is called the emergency control valve, or ECV. It is red. Check that it is working freely. When it is in line with the gas pipe it is on and when at right angles to it, the gas supply is isolated. If the handle is not easy to move, contact your utility provider and they will arrange a repair free of charge.

UTILITIES SUMMARY

Have a water stop tap installed within the property and ensure the tenants know its location.

Install an energy smart meter so you can choose the location.

Check the gas meter control valve (ECV) moves freely and advise the current gas supplier if it does not.

Take the meter readings on check-in and ensure there is a forwarding address for residual utility billing.

NOTES

17

FURNITURE INCLUDED IN INVENTORY

You can choose to provide whatever furniture you decide appropriate.

Sometimes tenants may only want their own furniture in the house but will accept the appliances in place.

Furniture supplied by you as the landlord must comply with fire regulations and the Furniture and Furnishings (Fire Safety) Regulations 1988. This is very important – even without incident a landlord can be fined £5,000 per item and imprisoned for up to 6 months just for providing items that do not meet the regulations.

Consequences of any incident within the rental property could be life-changing for a landlord.

My advice is, wherever possible, only supply furniture and appliances that will help to keep your target rent intact.

NOTES

18

PLUMBING

There are some areas you need to be aware of that can cause issues during a tenancy.

You should think about the possibility of issues with the plumbing system where leaks from the bath, basins, toilet, or the central heating system can cause damage to the fabric of the house.

BATH AND SINKS

Ensure the sealant between the bath and tiles/wall is intact and is not allowing any water egress under the bath. Also, if there is mould growth, clean it off or renew the sealant.

Check the taps work effectively and that they are solidly fixed to the bath or sink top.

If there are pop-up plugs fitted, leave a plunger in case the plugs become stuck closed. A quick pump on the plunger and the pop-up plug releases.

Leave at least one plunger at the property to encourage the tenant to clear blockages without resorting to contacting you or the managing agent.

SHOWER

If there is a standalone shower, check the sealant between the tray and the tiles is intact and free of mould. If there is mould on the sealant either clean it off or replace it. The tenant may request this as they may see it as unhygienic. If the sealant is clean when you rent the property and a request is received to have the mould removed during the tenancy, you will be within your rights to ask the tenant to pay for the work.

If there is an electric shower, ensure you have the make and model recorded in case repair or replacement becomes necessary. It is very common these days to replace rather than repair, given the replacement cost relative to a repair which may take more than one call-out by an engineer.

If there is a thermostatic shower, fed by hot water from the boiler, check the temperature and flow controls for ease of use. Should there be an issue with either of these controls, repair them before the property is rented.

If the shower is old or the valves do not work effectively, consider a replacement.

If you choose to have a new thermostatic shower installed, try and budget for a recognised brand rather than a trade-pack version, which will probably be what a plumber will offer to try to win the business. The problem with a lot of the trade packs is that most are imported with no spares supply chain and, if an issue arises out of warranty, your only option will be to replace it.

Recognised brands such as MIRA and Bristan will have an effective supply chain to provide spare parts for the shower. This will help reduce call-out charges to repair, should it be necessary, whilst a plumber may struggle to find spare parts for trade-pack versions.

One final point on showers. If you don't change the shower, consider changing the shower hose and head prior to the rental, as best practice, as these areas can be legionella breeding grounds. The cost of this change will be far less than the cost of a potential claim against you in the future.

ISOLATION VALVES

Consider installing isolation valves to the clean water feed pipe (hot and cold) close to a tap on a sink or bath or to a cistern. Most plumbers install these as a matter of course these days.

Why bother? If a tap or cistern develops a leak, isolating the supply at this point is much more effective than switching off the entire house supply at the stop tap, if one has been installed.

Isolation valves can be fitted into copper or plastic. The type for taps on baths and sinks tend to be fitted with flexible hoses leading from a copper or plastic pipe run to the tap.

WASTE OUTLETS

If you have any slow-running waste outlets such as sinks, baths, showers, or toilets then it may be worthwhile checking these out prior to the tenancy. If all is OK before the tenancy and an issue with drains comes up during the tenancy, then this could be handed back to the tenant, especially if only one outlet is affected. A blocked kitchen drain may be due to food and fat debris.

A blockage in the bath, shower, or bathroom sink is possibly due to soap or hair congestion. However, if there seems to be an issue with more than one outlet it may be that the soil pipe or external drains are blocked. In this case, it may be your responsibility to tackle the issue. If, after remedial action is taken, the blockage turns out to be caused by the tenant, such as from wet wipes or hair, then you would be within your rights to recharge.

Before rental, check the soil pipe at the same time you are checking the external gutters and downpipes.

LEGIONELLA

In domestic property rentals with combination boilers the risk from legionella is low, overall.

In properties with vented heating systems, cold water tanks are usually sited in the loft to feed water to the heating and hot water system. These types of systems can be a higher risk for legionella breeding potential.

Legionella needs water, air, and a warm environment to breed.

Water tanks should have tight-fitting lids to prevent debris falling into them.

Redundant pipework should be removed as this is where stagnant water can collect.

Keep the hot water system temperature at 60 degrees Celsius or above.

If your property has been empty for a period, you should flush the water system to get rid of stagnant water.

It may also be sensible to empty any water tanks if a property will be empty for a while.

In addition, if the property is empty for a period, change all shower heads and hoses as these can be a breeding ground for legionella, whether you have a combination boiler or a vented heating system.

Tenants should regularly clean showerheads and, where showers are not used regularly, tenants should be directed to disinfect the shower heads. This is more of an issue with thermostatic showers.

MACERATORS

If your rental property has a macerator for some waste outlets, clean it with a macerator cleaner prior to letting the property. This cleans and descales the macerator as it has a phosphoric acid base.

I recommend that you provide the tenant with a 5-litre container of macerator cleaner and advise the tenant to follow the instructions. If the property is supplied by hard water, it should be cleaned monthly and if the property is in a soft water area, it should be cleaned every 3 months. As the macerator processes waste from the tenant and family, it should be the tenant's responsibility to maintain it. You could legitimately advise them to buy their own cleaning fluid after the starter pack is used up.

The tenants should also be warned about the types of material that can be processed by a macerator. Only toilet paper. Everything else should be disposed of via a different channel.

Macerator call-outs tend to be more expensive than regular plumbing call-outs. Should a call-out be required for the macerator and the source of the issue is a blockage from disallowed materials then the tenant should reimburse you.

PLUMBING SUMMARY

Ensure sealant around baths or showers or sinks are in good condition – no gaps and no mould.

If budget allows, fit isolation valves to all possible water outlets, taps, cisterns, and baths.

Ensure all taps are easy to turn on and off and fixed firmly to the base.

Install a main stop tap to the property within the house. This is important.

Check that waste outlets run freely prior to rental.

Leave at least one plunger in the property.

NOTES

19

HEATING AND HOT WATER SYSTEMS

Heating and hot water systems can vary within any one property.

Around 80 per cent of properties in the UK have gas-fired central heating supplied either from a system or a combination boiler. A system boiler provides central heating in the same way as a combination boiler, but hot water is stored in a tank to distribute to tap outlets. Combination boilers provide instant hot water and central heating on demand.

Electric plus oil-fired heating forms a much smaller percentage of heating sources. These will be covered later.

I will not cover air or ground-source heating which has been headlined in political arenas recently.

BOILER SERVICING

Many landlords do not have boilers serviced every year for various reasons. Some think that the annual gas safety check is a service. Also, some managing agents do not see it as part of their remit to advise the landlord about the value of an annual boiler service.

Why have the boiler serviced annually?

First, if the boiler is under a manufacturer's warranty, it must be serviced annually in order for the warranty to be valid. I do not know of any manufacturer that does not stipulate this condition.

Second, to have the boiler serviced annually is the best way to guard against (as far as is reasonably possible) unexpected breakdown costs happening during the year that could cause emergency call-outs and extra costs.

In my experience boiler servicing is a good investment as I have seen extraordinary call-out costs for breakdowns that could have been avoided had a service been carried out. Some of those call-outs happen out of normal business hours, don't resolve the issue totally due to parts being required, and lead to further call-outs to repair the fault.

If the boiler has not been serviced during the previous 12 months before a new tenancy, ensure it is planned in at some point, even if it is after the tenant has moved in.

Boiler instructions

One of the recurring issues that has come up over time is the number of landlords who do not leave the boiler instruction set at the rental property. This can cause unnecessary calls to landlords or managing agents to assist the tenant to fire up the boiler, alter hot water and heating temperatures, or to reset the boiler. These operations are expected to be carried out by the householder, in this case, the tenant using the manufacturer's user instruction set.

If the tenant has the user instruction set and there is still a problem after they have carried out their checks, then a repair call can be actioned.

CENTRAL HEATING SYSTEM – THREE AREAS TO CHECK

At this point it may be worth discussing how a central heating system may be configured. This can help you to assist your new tenant on how to use the heating system effectively. I have found this is one area where new tenants find reasons to complain as they have difficulties understanding how to use the system. Often it leads to an engineer visit early on in the tenancy.

This next part is generally the same for heat-only boilers and combi boilers.

Central heating systems have three main areas from where the heating can be controlled.

The first is a heating programmer that enables timed periods for the heating to be set on or off. This heating programmer may be integral to the boiler or be wall-mounted within the house and may also be integrated with a thermostat control. If you have one on the boiler and a separate one in another location, set the boiler control to ON only, do not use the boiler integrated programmer. Use the wall-mounted programmer and thermostat.

A thermostat that controls the temperature in the room where it is sited (usually living room or hallway) can be used to bring the heating on by turning the temperature setting above the room's ambient temperature. As above, the thermostat may be integral with a programmer.

In older systems, the programmer may be remote from the thermostat, possibly built into the boiler, and be a mechanical version with pins to set the on and off periods.

Thermostatic Radiator Valves (TRVs) are the third control and are on radiators in individual rooms. They have settings between 0 and 5. There is usually an * setting above the 0 which has a set temperature around 7 degrees Celsius and should be used when the house is empty during a cold spell to keep a minimum temperature in the house. Usually there are valves on all but one radiator in the house to enable the water to flow around the system and back to the boiler, should all the valves be switched off. The bathroom towel radiator is the one that is often left without a valve or the room in which the thermostat is located.

Before rental, ensure the room thermostat is working effectively. Portable thermostats are usually powered by batteries. Change them for good measure. Check that all the thermostatic valves on radiators are working.

All settings on the boiler should be set by the boiler engineer at the time of service. Advise the tenant to leave the boiler heating settings as they are and use the TRVs and the heating thermostat or programmer to alter the heating.

The hot water control may be adjusted if it does not supply hot water at the required temperature.

Newer heating systems usually have a programmable thermostat which is a combined timer and thermostat.

This can either be fixed to a wall and wired to the boiler or it may be a portable version. This type of thermostat is usually sited in the main living area or in older installations in a hallway.

In addition, there may be TRVs fitted to all but one radiator. Ensure the programmable thermostat is working and change the batteries before rental.

RADIATORS AND PIPEWORK ISSUES

Central heating systems are made up of two parts: the boiler and the radiator system plus the associated pipework.

The radiator system is often neglected with all planned maintenance focused on the boiler.

As a central heating system ages, TRVs can leak and not work as effectively as they should to control the room temperature. These should be checked for leaks before the tenancy and that they actually control the temperature.

Radiators and the associated pipework can become saturated with debris from rust, known as sludge, that comes off the internal walls of radiators and from pipes and joints in the system and sits in an arc-like shape over the entire base of the radiator. This causes radiators to have cold spots, usually along their base and middle.

The other reason for cold spots on radiators is air in the system. This is probably due to air let in by microscopic holes at joints in the pipework. These increase in number as the system ages and gases form from corrosion of the internal surfaces of the system. Bleed the radiators as below to ensure they are free of air. WARNING! Householders should only bleed radiators when the heating is cold to prevent injury and to enable an accurate pressure reading to be taken at the boiler.

It is normally recommended that central heating systems are bled and topped up once per year to ensure optimum performance.

It is definitely worth checking the entire heating system for leaks and the effectiveness of each radiator. Bleed where necessary and if you notice a number of cold spots on radiators after bleeding, consider having the system flushed.

Bleeding radiators

Before you rent out your property, test the radiators for leaks and for even heating – no cold spots. If there are cold spots, this could indicate air in the system, so bleed them ahead of the start of the tenancy, especially if it is late summer or the beginning of autumn. It is possible that if the tenant moves in at this time of year they may ask for a heating engineer to visit on the basis that they would have expected the radiators to be in good working order at the start of the tenancy.

Air bubbles form in radiators over time for various reasons and so bleeding radiators is a normal expected tenant activity during the tenancy. Good practice will be to leave a radiator key at the property for the tenant to use. They can be bought very cheaply at hardware shops or online.

Cold spots on radiators could cause the tenant to try to turn the thermostat up to compensate. This may have no effect on the heating but might affect the tenant's heating bills.

If you bleed the radiators, it is likely that the boiler pressure will need to be raised as you have taken air pressure out of the system.

SLUDGE AND DEBRIS IN THE CENTRAL HEATING SYSTEM

As discussed, sludge can also affect the heating effectiveness of the radiator system and boiler performance. The sludge can affect the heat pump and valves within the boiler and the sludge-ridden water can deplete the overall heating effectiveness of the boiler as less heat is transferred to the water as it travels past the heat exchanger due to its density.

Periodically, especially as systems age, it may be pertinent to have the system flushed. When a system is flushed a chemical is added to water and fed into the pipework. This flushes the sludge and debris to an exit pipe where it is channelled to a drain.

If you have a warranty on your boiler, the manufacturer may stipulate a system flush be carried out at the time the boiler is installed as part of the warranty conditions. If no flush is carried out and sludge subsequently causes an issue it may void the warranty.

CONDENSATE PIPE

Most combination boilers these days are condensing boilers and wastewater is produced as part of the operation. This is normally discharged internally into the waste pipe of a sink, bath, or shower, or directly into the internal soil pipe. Alternatively, it may be routed externally through a pipe which can be seen on an external wall where the boiler is sited. Do not be confused by another pipe which is situated externally with a short piece of pipe showing. This is the pressure relief valve discharge outlet. The condensate pipe should run down to a drain and be at least 32 mm in diameter. The reason for the minimum pipe size is to allow for the volume of water that a boiler gives off (approximately 2 litres per hour when working) to reach the drain without freezing and blocking the pipe in cold weather.

Wrapping the condensate pipe in suitable external pipe insulation is a good idea. This may not be effective in very cold weather, however, and sometimes a tenant may have to resort to pouring warm water over the pipe. In the worst case scenario, if a condensate pipe is partially blocked and water backs up into the boiler system it could cause damage to components. Pipe insulation is relatively inexpensive but a damaged boiler will incur a much higher repair cost.

One last point on condensate pipes. If the pipe from the boiler to the drain is less than 32 mm in diameter, say 22 mm, consider replacing it with a larger one. Having a pipe that meets the regulation size would prevent the pipe from freezing up and eliminate the consequent damage that could occur. The cost to make this change is relatively small compared to an engineer call-out or a void warranty claim. Should an issue result from the blockage of the condensate pipe it may affect an associated warranty claim.

RE-PRESSURISING THE BOILER

This is not a part of the property preparation, but it will help you be aware of how to re-pressurise the boiler in your rental property.

This is a very common issue that arises in tenanted properties and occurs when the pressure in the boiler system drops causing the boiler to fail to ignite.

There may be a pressure gauge integral to the boiler, or one installed by the installation engineer on the pipework below the boiler. This is the first place to look after checking any digital or display for error codes if the boiler will not ignite.

If the pressure gauge is sitting below 0.5 the boiler will probably not ignite. This is a general rule of thumb, and each model of boiler will have different pressure-setting thresholds below which the boiler will fail to work.

To re-pressurise the boiler there may be an inbuilt filling loop on the boiler to introduce water into the system. Follow the boiler instructions to top up the pressure. Alternatively, there may be a braided stainless-steel hose linking two copper pipes under the boiler with either one or two taps, one at either end of the loop. The loop may also be copper instead of stainless steel. Generally, look for two vertical copper pipes linked by a pipe and with one or two taps. One vertical pipe will be the mains water inlet pipe and the other will be the pipe to the boiler. Once you know where the filling loop is located, keep one eye on the pressure gauge and open one of the taps slowly; if there is only one tap then opening this will start to introduce water into the boiler. If there are two taps, then open the second tap more slowly to control the water flow into the boiler. Once the pressure gauge reaches 1.5 bar, close off both taps or the one that you opened. Just for reference, the taps are usually open when the lever is in line with the pipe and closed when at right angles to the connected pipe. It is possible the taps may not be present and there will be flat-head screwdriver slots into which you can insert a screwdriver or knife blade and turn to control the water flow.

I would strongly recommend that this process be documented and left with the instruction sets passed to the new tenant.

If the boiler does not have a filling loop, then I would also strongly recommend having one fitted before renting out the property. Should the boiler need re-pressurising and you or the managing agent are not able to talk a tenant through this process on the phone or by messaging, it could end up with a heating contractor call-out. The average call-out cost is £60 to £100 and if there is no filling loop then the cost for an installation could be up to another £150 to £200. Do not bypass this warning. At least 50 per cent of call-outs due to loss of boiler pressure can be avoided if a filling loop is present.

Finally, in my experience tenants cannot find the filling loop without assistance due to boilers having multiple pipes and valves underneath. Label or tag the filling loop!

Should you consider a new boiler?

As a boiler ages, parts start to fail and once a boiler starts needing age-related repairs it can start to deteriorate as engineers disturb other parts that then fault or fail.

If the boiler is approaching 8 to 10 years old, it may be pertinent to consider planning a replacement boiler at some point rather than wait for repairs to creep in and eat into your budget.

The best time to replace a boiler is in between tenancies to reduce disruption unless an incident during the tenancy forces a replacement. One idea is to set a budget for repairs and if exceeded, consider planning a new boiler. A fair warning figure for repairs may be £500, given the average cost of a new boiler is £2,000 plus. Also, factor in the age of the boiler. This is a guide.

If there is a system boiler in place and the new boiler is to be a combination boiler, you will need to consider the removal of the associated tanks for cold and hot water. Pipework alteration may also be necessary.

New combination boilers can come with up to a 12-year warranty.

Payment plans can assist you to offset the boiler's capital cost plus annual services over either the life of the boiler or a period to suit your finances.

In industry in general, operational equipment is often bought on a rental or lease basis, and the cost is offset against sales income, so why not do the same for a property rental?

A boiler and central heating system are probably the second-largest planned investment costs that a landlord will make in any one property.

If you are considering renewing the boiler system, then you should be aware that changes have been made to new boiler installation regulations and the following will now be required at the same time as the boiler installation: thermostatic radiator valves added or replaced, if faulty, and a new programmer and thermostat, hardwired or wireless. The central heating system will need to be flushed, a rust inhibitor added, and a magnet filter installed to extract the sludge created by corrosion that occurs in the radiators and pipework as the water passes through. This work will help to protect your new boiler investment as well as improve the effectiveness of the central heating system over the longer term.

LPG (Liquified Petroleum Gas) fired boilers

These are treated in exactly the same way as a natural gas boiler and are covered by the same regulations.

Oil heating

An oil boiler does exactly what a gas boiler does. The fuel is the only difference. Oil is a dirty fuel. They can become contaminated with water and cause the boiler to stop working.

Oil boilers do not need an annual check by law. However, I recommend that any oil boiler be serviced every year to lessen the chances of emergency call-outs. If you are working with a managing agent, ensure this service is planned in. It is unlikely to come up on their radar as it is not a legal requirement. I know several landlords that never think about having their rental property oil boilers serviced.

Oil-fired central heating systems should be treated the same as their gas-fired boiler counterparts.

ELECTRIC HEATING AND HOT WATER SYSTEMS

If the property has either storage heaters or electric panel heaters, ensure they are all working and an instruction set copy is left at the property.

Immersion tanks for hot water may have two controls to provide hot water either on the overnight electricity rate (economy rate) or on the day rate sometimes labelled 'boost' on the programmer. If they do not have these then they could be on a simple timer that is either mechanical or digital.

Some tenants find these programmers confusing to operate and in my own experience I have found that some tenants have been using boost instead of the cheaper overnight electricity as they didn't know or understand how to operate the programmer.

I recommend that you leave an instruction set on how to operate the hot water system and if there are quirks to using it effectively that you prepare a set of instructions to assist the tenant.

CHIMNEYS

If the property has chimneys and they are used for either solid-fuel heating or gas appliances, then the landlord is responsible for their maintenance.

If there is more than one chimney but only one is nominated to be used for solid fuel, then make this clear within the tenancy agreement. You are responsible to have this cleaned once per year. If there are other chimney openings in the property that are not used, seal them off to prevent draughts. Install a chimney balloon or have a handyman seal it off completely.

In the case of a chimney used for solid-fuel heating, the tenant can choose to have it swept more than once a year at their cost unless there is a technical issue that requires it to be swept more frequently.

Chimney sweeps are like gold dust between September and Christmas. Book ahead.

HEATING AND HOT WATER SYSTEMS SUMMARY

If there is gas to the property, ensure the tenant is given a current annual gas certificate on check-in and on every anniversary as soon as the annual gas check is completed.

Plan in an annual service on the boiler and a central heating check.

Leave an instruction set for boiler use at the property or give the tenant a data key including all appliance instructions sets.

Check that boiler controls are in working order.

Check all radiator valves (TRVs) are working.

Check room thermostats are working and change batteries if necessary.

Check radiators for even heating across the radiator surface and bleed if necessary.

If, after bleeding, the radiators still have cold spots, consider a system flush to remove the debris and installation of a magnetic filter to prevent sludge from affecting the system and boiler in the future.

If the boiler condensate pipe has an external run, insulate with pipe insulation.

Find out how to re-pressurise the boiler and leave an instruction set at the property or place on a data key with the other appliance instructions.

If there is no filling loop to re-pressurise the boiler, install one and label it so it is easy to locate.

Leave a radiator bleed key at the property.

If heating and hot water is electrical then ensure instruction sets for both the heating and the hot water systems are left at the property.

If there is a working fireplace, book a chimney sweep in advance of autumn.

Consider sharing a google document that you can update at any point instead of leaving a data key or document copies. This may be easier to administer if you replace appliances or have works done mid tenancy that may require tenant input or maintenance.

NOTES

20

DRAINS

It is often confusing about who is responsible for drains leading to public sewers from detached houses, semi-detached, terraced houses, and blocks of flats.

I feel it is wise to mention this now –not that anything needs doing ahead of your first rental, but it is worth checking what the drain situation is to assist you to manage issues if they arise and cut out wasted call-out costs.

Since 2011 it has become much easier to know who is responsible for drains.

The local water company is responsible for what are termed lateral drains and the public sewer system. A lateral drain is a publicly owned drain that is usually on private property or between a property boundary and the public sewer system.

You, as the property owner are responsible for the drain that runs from the building on your property to the property boundary and everything inside the house.

This is easy for detached houses. There should only be a drain cover on the public pavement area.

Usually, you will be responsible for the drain to the manhole nearest the public sewer. However, if you have a drain within the bounds of your property this may indicate it is part of a system servicing other houses. If your property is detached and there is a drain cover in your garden, open it and check if there is a pipe running into it from the direction of an adjacent property. Then, check if there is an inlet from your property and an outlet towards the public pavement. If this is the case then it is possible an issue in the manhole on your property may be covered by the local water authority. So, if a blockage issue arises you could call the water authority first, ask them for advice on who owns the drain, and see if they will attend rather than employ a drainage contractor.

For flats, the block landlord is responsible for the drains from the building to the boundary plus communal soil pipes within the building. Issues that arise in the communal soil pipes may lead back to an individual flat. If this happens, the block management company will probably negotiate with the individual flat owners based on the lease agreement. Individual flat owners will be responsible for the drains that run from their flats to the joint with the communal block soil pipe.

Terraces and semi-detached houses are slightly different. Working back from the boundary, where the public manhole is sited on entry to the sewer system, all drains are the water authority's responsibility back to the boundary of the first terrace or semi-detached in the run (the one furthest from the public manhole). The property at the beginning of the run is responsible for their own drains up to the first neighbouring boundary.

DRAINS SUMMARY

Check the drain status before renting out the property. Call the local water company. This can save you money as you may be eligible to call the local water company to handle drain issues depending upon where your rental property is located in the drains network.

Ensure drain responsibility information is distributed to the tenant and managing agent.

NOTES

21

DAMP

With the rising number of disrepair claims in the UK it is worth discussing the different types of damp here, in order for you to be aware of the possible issues and causes and to be forearmed in case damp issues arise in your rental property.

First, if you are aware of any damp issues that exist already, check to see if you need to take action before your tenant checks in.

Rising, penetrating, and condensation damp are all issues that can affect a property and cause frustrations during a tenancy to both you as a landlord and your tenant.

Reported damp-related issues in tenanted properties are becoming more prevalent, partly due to the rise of 'no win no fee' solicitors entering the arena driven by these issues in social housing.

But this is not to advise that you should only look at them due to legal risks. If there is structural damp or a possible risk of condensation damp, it is best to review these now and plan in works or householder processes to prevent them from becoming an issue.

In private rented housing, the main type of reported damp is condensation-based damp which can be largely down to the living conditions of the tenant. There can be other contributory circumstances that can agitate condensation damp which could be resolved if it is acknowledged that it would have a positive effect on reducing condensation damp.

Rising and penetrating damp are issues that need structural intervention as discussed below.

RISING DAMP

This affects ground-floor rooms. It can come from a damaged damp proof course. It can also be the result of external works that have altered the ground level next to the property where an increase in ground height, possibly from a new path or soil added to a garden bed, has meant that the top of the new surface sits above the damp proof course allowing moisture into the mortar and brickwork. There are other potential causes such as damaged underground drains.

The effects of rising damp will be a damp area rising from the floor or skirting board level. This will have an effect on the wall fabric over time so this is best tackled as early as possible.

PENETRATING DAMP

This can come from external issues, usually above ground level, and could be related to gutter, downpipe, or soil pipe leaks or wall issues such as damaged mortar, porous brick or stone, or possibly wall cavity issues, as well as door or window-frame sealant issues. It manifests itself internally as damp patches off floor level and as efflorescence showing through on the internal wall surface or blown plaster. Leaks from roofs are considered as penetrating damp and appear as damp patches on the ceiling.

Penetrating damp can look worse during and shortly after wet weather as water ingress becomes more concentrated. The damp patches may feel wet to the touch.

CONDENSATION DAMP

This is a complex area and often there is a divide in opinion between tenants, landlords, agents, and even specialists about what causes condensation build-up and the consequent mould damage in any one property.

I have been part of several council investigations where, at the end of the assessment, the finger of blame is pointed at the tenant for not carrying out householder duties as expected to eliminate condensation by adequate heating and ventilation practices.

On the other hand, landlords have been advised that had they installed other ventilation facilities such as fan units in bathrooms and kitchens, the effects of condensation-based issues would have been reduced by a greater extent.

Then there is the fact that tenants and householders in general do not understand the underlying causes of condensation damp.

My experience seems to illustrate that tenants treat or manage a property differently than a homeowner may do. They do not always understand the need to properly ventilate and heat a house to prevent moisture build-up.

Sometimes condensation damp could be reduced, especially in older houses if 'cold walls' were better insulated to prevent the temperature of the internal surface of external walls becoming lower than the temperature of other surrounding internal walls. Cold walls attract warm moisture which condenses on the relatively cold surface. As this cools, bacteria grow and mould is formed.

Finally, the effects of condensation are rarely simple but much could be mitigated if the tenant used available extraction facilities, used trickle vents on windows, opened windows more readily and used heating to keep the ambient temperature in the house steady.

If you have noticed condensation mould build-up whilst living in the property or at the time of the property purchase, you may want to consider having this treated by a specialist firm before rental. Be aware if you ignore a possible issue like this it may become an area the tenant may raise at a future point when condensation starts to appear. There are specialist firms that can assist you with condensation damp analysis and routes to alleviate the issue.

Here are some key points to know about managing condensation:

- Drying clothes indoors produces the most moisture – around 35 per cent of the total moisture produced daily in a home.
- Cooking produces around 20 to 25 per cent of the total.
- Two people at home for 16 hours per day produces around 10 to 15 per cent of the total.
- One bath or shower or washing up produces around 7 to 10 per cent of the daily total.

If your property is prone to condensation, prepare ahead as I have mentioned above.

If remedial works are not affordable, consider providing a window vac to assist the tenant with daily clearance of moisture build-up overnight. Most condensation will settle on the windows as they tend to be the coldest surfaces. Daily clearance will help alleviate the moisture being penetrated by bacteria and turning to mould.

Given that drying clothes produces the majority of condensation, consider installing a condensing dryer or a model that has a hose that vents to the outside. Also, provide an external clothes line or rotary dryer to encourage drying clothes outside.

Most householders install 'over hob' hoods which are purely filters that absorb odours and grease. Consider a ducted extractor hood as this will literally suck the moisture out of the kitchen.

To work out what size fan you need with the extractor, measure the height, width, and length of the kitchen in metres. This will give you the cubic metreage. Multiply this figure by 10. This will give you cubic metres per hour. When you are reviewing fans, look for a fan that meets that extraction rate.

Alternatively, instead of an extractor hood you could install an extractor fan using the same principles above.

To help increase the moisture extraction even more, consider a humidity-controlled extractor. This will remain on until the moisture level drops to the level pre-set on the fan. The sensitivity of the humidity control can usually be manually altered.

An extractor hood should be considered over a fan unit because most moisture produced in a kitchen is produced during cooking.

To choose a bathroom fan with an adequate extraction rate, multiply the room volume in metres by 7. This will give you the cubic litres per hour. This is slightly above the building regulations advised level. Look for fans that meet that extraction rate.

For your information, in the UK we work on cubic metres per hour. In the US they work on cubic feet per hour. If you find fans with cubic feet per hour specified, then multiply the figure by 0.03 to arrive at the cubic metre extraction rate.

There are many guidance documents available online for householders to manage condensation.

If you decide to build a Household Management Document as described in Section 26, you may want to include some guidance as follows:

- Ensure the fan is on when cooking;
- Keep the kitchen door closed when cooking;
- Keep lids on saucepans when cooking;
- Keep the bathroom door closed when bathing or showering;
- Wipe up excess moisture on cold surfaces after showering, bathing, or cooking;
- Wipe moisture off windows daily;
- Use a bath mat to absorb moisture after a bath or shower;
- Keep all furniture away from external walls to allow air to flow rather than create a trap where moisture can settle onto relatively cold surfaces;

- Do not overfill wardrobes with clothes as air will not be able to circulate and will settle on the clothes producing mildew;
- Ensure windows are opened regularly, especially in the mornings to disperse accumulated moisture; and
- Use a clothes dryer to dry clothes or hang them outside to dry.

If you feel you have done the best you can to reduce the risks of condensation, bear in mind the information above to assist you should issues arise during the tenancy.

Given that condensation damp is a hot topic, I would recommend you act fast when it is reported. Document the report and any analysis of the causes along with photos in case these are required by any third party investigation by bodies such as the environmental section of the local council.

DAMP SUMMARY

Review the property for signs of damp prior to renting it out. If possible, ensure these issues are tackled.

Check external walls for pointing damage or moss growing in the mortar joints which may indicate a gutter or downpipe issue where water is falling onto the wall causing moss to develop.

To reduce the risks of condensation damp, consider humidity-controlled fans in the kitchen and bathrooms.

If condensation damp has been an issue in your rental property, seek advice from a specialist.

Consider a window vac to remove moisture daily.

Provide the tenant with clear information on how to prevent condensation.

NOTES

22

BURGLAR ALARMS

Should you decide to offer a burglar alarm as part of your property rental, you should consider having it serviced prior to rental to ensure the system and sensors are in working order. The tenant and any managing agent should be aware of the setup process and any operating codes. An instruction set should also be provided to enable the tenant to use it competently. This will prevent you from being subject to unnecessary calls and call-outs to undertake resets or setups that could have been resolved by the tenant.

The single biggest issue with burglar alarms is when the alarm has been left in place, not checked or serviced, no instruction set left, and no one is given the access code. The tenant tries to use the system, the alarm goes off, and they can't disable it. Or the power goes down and the alarm goes off on when the power comes back on. The average call-out cost for this issue is approximately £65 to £125, possibly more if it is an out-of-hours call-out.

My advice is, if the alarm adds nothing to the rental value, think seriously about having it disabled; otherwise, it is just another system to manage. The appearance of the external box should have the same effect as a working alarm to deter would-be burglars.

If you still want to include the alarm as part of a rental, have it serviced and possibly put a service contract in place to have it serviced annually or bi-annually and agree with the same company to carry out repairs should the alarm go faulty. I would also suggest that the alarm unit be labelled with the service agent details in case of overnight incidents, to prevent you or the managing agent from having to manage these situations.

Should a call-out to the alarm be traced to user error and you have supplied all operational details, you should charge the tenant.

BURGLAR ALARM SUMMARY

If you are offering a burglar alarm with the rental, consider having it serviced.

Leave details of a suitable service agent in case of an out-of-hours issue.

NOTES

23

PESTS

How you as a landlord deal with pest issues will depend upon the nature of the incident.

If a pest enters the property through an entry point in the fabric of the building then maybe you should accept this as your responsibility.

Before you rent out the property, look around externally and internally for entry points such as pipe boxing, under kickboards in the kitchen, or in the loft space or cellar/basement areas. Seal any likely entry points prior to the rental.

Check door thresholds for gaps and seal these.

Should pests be reported by your tenant, think about the report in common-sense terms. Is this something you could have prevented? Is this pest incident related to a failure of the fabric of the property? If it is, accept responsibility and action it.

Areas of controversy are moths, fleas, bees, wasps, flying insects, and bed bugs.

If moths migrate from outside, then is this really the landlord's fault? It is probably due to open windows and doors, the moths being drawn to lights, and proximity of trees and garden areas to where they eat. I recommend you advise the tenant to handle the issue. The only time you may want to take responsibility is when it happens shortly after the start of the tenancy. At this point, it may be considered that the issue predated the new tenancy.

Fleas and bed bugs. Fleas can be associated with dogs and cats or any animal with fur where they can settle and multiply. Bed bugs can be transported in travel bags and cases from other sources such as hotels. If there is an incidence of this mid-tenancy, pass the issue back to the tenant. If it occurs at the start, say within 4 weeks, take responsibility.

Bees, wasps, and other flying insects may come from several sources. If a bee's or wasp's nest is housed in the loft or attached to the property, you should tackle the issue. If the nest is in a tree or a garden shed, then ask the tenant to take responsibility as a householder.

For other flying insects, treat the same as above. Fly infestations could be down to food being left uncovered. They may also be due to generally unhygienic living conditions.

Other external causes of flying insect infestations are bins being left open with waste food and packaging not having been sealed before disposal.

Don't automatically accept responsibility. Remember the householder concept. A tenant is a householder as well and they have householder management responsibilities too.

PESTS SUMMARY

Seal any entry points on the external walls as well as any interior walls such as under kickboards.

Consider any reports from the tenant carefully. Ask yourself 'Is this pest situation caused by something I have failed to do?' If the answer is no, there may be grounds to advise the tenant to take responsibility for the issue.

NOTES

24

PETS

To date pets have been an area of controversy for both landlords and tenants.

Landlords have been able to refuse pets based on personal considerations. Less than 10 per cent of UK landlords actually have provisions for pets in their tenancy agreements.

The law is changing in favour of pet owners.

First, the government's model assured shorthold tenancy template has been altered to include a clause in favour of tenants keeping pets as long as they apply in writing and that there are no valid reasons to refuse permission, such as the pet being too large for the property. If you as a landlord do not respond within 28 days, the tenant has an automatic right to house the pet.

Currently, this is only if you have used the government's model tenancy agreement and if you have left this clause in place.

To add to this, the Dogs and Domestic Animals (Accommodation Protection) Bill aims to further protect the welfare of domestic animals.

This upcoming legislation will assist pet owners to get around the fact that the take-up of the model tenancy agreement has been much lower than expected so pet ownership in rental properties is still being stifled. However, the new laws will also give landlords rights too.

Tenants will need to gain a certificate of responsible ownership; basically, certified by a vet and covering requirements such as microchipping where feasible, appropriate vaccinations, and their pet's ability to respond to basic commands.

Once they have this certificate, landlords will have limited reasons for not allowing a tenant to keep pets.

As a landlord you will have rights to prevent tenants keeping pets based on certain criteria such as suitability of property but you will need to hold a certificate of exemption for the rental property.

A landlord will be able to charge for pet damage but it is not clear currently whether a premium may be chargeable if a tenant applies for a tenancy with a pet.

This will be an area to keep an eye on. The private rental sector and the veterinary sector will work at different paces so it is not clear how long it will be until a clear working system will be in place.

PETS SUMMARY

Upcoming legislation - Renters' Reform Bill is in its early stages and will aim to move the balance to tenants' having the right to keep a suitable pet in the accommodation they live in or plan to make their home. Landlords must seriously consider any requests, and the landlord will not be able to refuse unreasonably.

If you do not want pets in your property, you will need a valid reason why they cannot be housed there.

Ensure you answer any pet-related correspondence within 28 days of receipt or the tenant gains an automatic right to keep the pet in question at the property.

NOTES

25

TRADESMEN AND CONTRACTORS

If you are renting your house directly (not through a managing agent) and are not DIY competent or if you live a distance from your rental property, build a team of contractors you can call on to provide services covering the following areas, and who can be available within the lead times you will need to meet your landlord obligations.

If possible, try to find a handyman who can cover most small to medium jobs from basic plumbing issues to changing light pendants to curtain or blind issues.

An electrician and plumber will be useful in case of major issues arise such as loss of power and leaks. If you can find a plumber who is also a heating engineer this can be very useful as issues with either gas boilers, central heating systems, or immersion heaters are common. It will also be valuable to ensure your choice of plumber or heating engineer is familiar with the make and model of the heating and hot water system in the property.

Also, find a builder who can tackle more major issues that the handyman cannot fulfil.

Agreeing to rates and attendance lead times should be a primary part of your conversation with your team. This will be important to ensure you can respond within acceptable timeframes and keep your budget under control.

The agreement should also include out-of-hours call-out possibilities to ensure issues such as loss of power, uncontrollable leaks, or loss of heating can be tackled in short order, to help you meet your obligations.

Should you be renting through a managing agent and you have a competent team of tradesmen who can provide good service delivery, ensure the agent adds them to your landlord profile so these tradesmen can be approached ahead of any agent-led contractor. It is possible that your tradesmen may not be available if the issue is reported as an emergency, so the agent may have to appoint their own contractor to ensure the emergency is handled appropriately but, at least for most situations, you will be in control of the repairs.

TRADESMEN AND CONTRACTORS SUMMARY

If you are managing your own rental property, build a team of competent tradesmen that fit your budget and who can meet deadlines required to fulfil your obligations.

If you are working with a managing agent and have your own team, ensure the agent has your contractor contact details to work with them, including email, mobile numbers, and availability.

NOTES

26

TENANCY HOUSEHOLD MANAGEMENT

Given today's increasingly 'demanding' approach by tenants and an increasingly claims-driven sector, you as a landlord should not be afraid to document property-specific processes and requirements to present and discuss with prospects and the new tenant on check-in.

This may help you later if you are required to produce documents to illustrate how you have prepared the house for rental and provided good household management information to the tenant.

First, you need to be clear what you want in your tenancy agreement that is specific to your property. As previously discussed, this can be placed in an addendum to the standard agreement.

Second, prepare a Household Management Document into which you may want to build tenant tasks and responsibilities, some of which you may have added to the tenancy agreement addendum.

The idea of this document is for it to be a pragmatic working instrument for the tenant to use to manage the property effectively from a householder stance. This is a laborious job but could pay dividends during the tenancy.

The Household Management Document could include processes to be undertaken as described below. It could also include all the user instruction sets for appliances and handy tips such as how to re-pressurise the boiler. The document could be handed over on a data key or shared on a Google document. The latter method would make updating between tenancies more practical.

You may think that if you are going to work with a managing agent they will take care of this. Wrong! They will have their own tenancy agreement template. You will need to furnish them with anything else that you want included. Trust me when I say this. This is one of the most important jobs you have to do as part of the business of preparing to let your property and you or a trusted third party need to execute this.

The Household Management Document should be an easily understandable set of processes and instructions so that the new tenant will know what is expected of them whilst a tenant in your property.

If you are working with an agent, ensure they have a copy prior to viewings so that the contents can be discussed with prospective tenants at that stage.

An idea of how to kick-start the document is below:

Start with a simple list, maybe by room or location.

For instance, start in the garden and list the shrubs and hedges to be managed by you and those to be managed by the tenant.

Internally, for example in the kitchen, list the processes to be carried out such as checking and cleaning the washing machine and dishwasher filters regularly.

Additionally, cleaning or changing the extractor filters would also be included.

If you leave a window vac to help clear condensation moisture, advise the frequency that you recommend this process is carried out, to lessen the chance that moisture will grow bacteria.

Include boiler and heating control processes. Include instruction sets on how to operate the boiler and central heating system. The boiler instructions may include how to top up the pressure and how to use the boiler controls.

Information for bleeding radiators should be part of the document. You could leave a radiator key and advise that the tenant should bleed the radiators if cold spots occur in any of them.

Other instructions to be provided would be:

- Checking the filter, bag, and suction hose on vacuum cleaners, if supplied.
- Replacing light bulbs and batteries in smoke detectors.
- Replacing electrical fuses.
- Using a plunger and drain cleaner for blocked drains before calling for assistance.
- Keeping food in suitable containers or cupboards and not lying around as this may encourage vermin.
- Keeping extractor fans free from dust and grease.
- Regularly opening windows to ventilate the property. This could help later if an issue arises such as condensation and you had included ventilation as a crucial part of the household management process, to disperse moisture from the property.

- Changing extractor fan filters when they become congested with grease and debris.

If possible, get a signature from the tenant so that they concur with the Household Management Document. This will assist you, should anything happen that could have been averted by the tenant taking appropriate action.

TENANCY HOUSEHOLD MANAGEMENT SUMMARY

Consider placing all processes to be carried out by the tenant into a document that you can refer back to if an issue arises that could be because the tenant did not properly manage the process (e.g. washing machine blockage due to a congested filter).

Have this document available for prospects and as part of the check-in process.

Sign it and have the tenant countersign it.

Give a copy to the managing agent to discuss with prospects and at check-in.

NOTES

27

INSURANCE

This is an area worth discussing for both you as a landlord and to assist you in discussions with your tenant.

LANDLORD INSURANCE

There is no legal requirement for landlords to have insurance cover of any sort on rental property unless certain mortgages such as buy-to-let require it as part of their lending criteria.

Why bother to take out cover then? There are many issues that can arise where a landlord's insurance policy will be valuable.

I would strongly recommend having landlord insurance on any rental property to cover the following:

- Accidental damage such as roof failures on both pitched and flat roofs. Storm-damaged roofs can have far-reaching consequences other than just immediate roof damage. Internal water damage to walls, ceilings, flooring, and personal items can be extensive.
- Water damage from pipe leaks. Water is not discriminatory about where it flows and what it damages. Leaks from burst joints can destroy floors, wall coverings, and ceilings. One factor to be aware of is that some insurance policies have separate excesses for water leaks and the excess may be as high as £1,000.
- Fire can affect an entire property with smoke and fire damage to the fabric of the property and personal items.

If the damage is extensive it may be worthwhile working with an insurance management company to handle the claim with your insurer. See details below.

Do not bypass investment in this type of policy. I am saying this as some landlords don't obtain a suitable policy for letting out their property. Some fail to tell their current insurer that they are now landlords and think that their current buildings and contents policies will cover them. In the majority of cases it won't.

The value of a good policy will outstrip the cost should you need to call on it.

At a basic level, if you were living in your rental property, you would probably opt for buildings insurance because a mortgage required it or because you wanted to protect the fabric of your home. You would probably have a contents policy too.

Your rental property is an income-earning asset, and you should at least protect the basics. This will not protect you from your property maintenance responsibilities (roofs, guttering, drains, etc) but will assist you in the event of unforeseen events happening.

If a leak happens through a roof during a storm and it is established that a freak wind had caused the damage, then you would probably be covered for the roof repair and any associated leak damage.

However, if the rainstorm caused water to force its way through failed mortar on the ridge, then you would probably have to pay for the roof repair and the insurer would pay for the internal damage.

Should the house become uninhabitable for a period, say, due to fire or flood, some policies will cover you for alternative accommodation for the tenants. In addition, if the property is empty in between tenancies and an incident occurs, this can be covered too.

I recommend that you consider the following areas be covered on your landlord insurance.

Fixtures and fittings that you have provided such as carpets, floor coverings, curtains, light fittings, windows, doors, and white goods. This would not exclude you being able to charge the tenant, should they cause damage to any contents, but should enable you to claim for flood or fire damage if you could not get reimbursed for accidental damage from the tenant, for whatever reason.

A policy that has additional cover for fire or flood damage and the excess costs of re-housing your tenants whilst the property is brought back to a habitable condition is worth considering.

Each element you add to a policy will increase the cost, but the key is balancing the policy cost against the risk and consequent management cost should a claimable event occur. In effect, you are paying for the best future financial outcome in the event of a serious incident and peace of mind.

There is also rent guarantee insurance which seems to have become more popular since the start of the pandemic of 2020. This is cover for when an incumbent tenant may not be able to pay all or part of the rent. This insurance type has proved valuable recently as landlords think about the consequence of a tenant not being able to pay the rent and the difficulty in evicting them in the short term for both legal and moral reasons.

The insurance elements above are ones that I have seen landlords use effectively to ensure adequate cover for their rental property.

If you are working with a managing agent, you should be able to ask them to handle any insurance claims on your behalf as long as you advise your insurers that is your preference.

One last thing to consider in the event of a serious event such as a fire or flood. Consider using a claims management company to manage the claim with your insurers.

An insurance claims management company will project manage the entire claim from start to finish. They will handle all communication with your insurers, agree scope of works, arrange the works, manage any temporary rehousing of tenants, sign off all the works, and reinstate your tenants in the property on completion.

This is a well-trodden path and negates you having to find time to manage the situation.

These heroes are paid for by your insurer and are worth their weight in gold!

INSURANCE FOR FLAT RENTALS

If you own and rent out a flat in a block then you are probably the leaseholder. In this case you should have a landlord policy to cover insurance issues that arise within the flat. Should an incident occur within the block that originated within your flat then there should be a block building insurance policy that will cover most issues in communal areas or other flats. If there is any reclaim due against your property, then the building insurer will contact you or the tenant for recompense after the damage has been repaired. You will be responsible for the repair in your property. Perhaps your tenant left the tap running water into a bath and it overflowed into a third-party flat. In this case the tenant is liable and the building insurer would normally refer to them for recompense for any damage caused to the other flat. They may try to reclaim the costs from you or your insurer if the claim against the tenant is not fruitful. Obviously, you will be within your rights to claim the costs for the repairs in your property from the tenant during the tenancy or from the deposit if they are proved to be responsible.

The other areas where insurance can assist you is if one of the tenants is injured and it is considered you are at fault.

TENANT CONTENTS INSURANCE

There is a general misunderstanding about who is responsible if tenant possessions are damaged in various circumstances during the tenancy.

I know of tenants who have asked landlords to pay for damage to their personal possessions such as vehicles damaged by fencing being blown down, computers and other items damaged by leaks, and items stolen after a break-in.

This is generally unreasonable and outside most, if not all, tenancy agreement terms. If a landlord has provided a safe, well-maintained property for a tenant and an accident occurs or there is a break-in, the landlord's responsibility is to ensure that any damage to the property is repaired. If any furnishings or items supplied on the inventory are damaged, then they should also be repaired or replaced.

The tenant as a householder should have contents insurance, as they would in their own property, to cover their belongings.

Ask yourself this: If a tenant was in a mortgaged property and there was a leak that damaged their belongings, would they ask the mortgage company to pay out? No! A mortgage is, in its basic form, a long-term rental.

Over 60 per cent of tenants do not have insurance cover but, in the general housing market, only around 25 per cent of all households do not have insurance. The two main reasons are that householders or tenants either cannot afford it or they don't think they will need it. However, that does not automatically transfer responsibility to the landlord for damage to a tenant's belongings.

I strongly recommend that you encourage your tenants to get contents insurance and if you are working with a managing agent then task them with this job.

Advise the tenant that if an accident – be that a leak, flood, fire, or theft – were to happen, then you will cover the cost of repairs but should any of their contents be damaged they will be responsible for the repairs or replacements directly or through their insurance policy.

One area worth further note is what happens after a break-in or burglary.

The tenant may want to leave the tenancy early if they feel unsafe or uncomfortable remaining in the property. You can choose if you want to charge the tenant for the period up to the end of the originally agreed tenancy date, or you could choose to charge administrative fees to match what it costs you to release the incumbent tenant and acquire a new tenant plus the rent up to the date the new tenants check in.

After a break-in or burglary a tenant may want extra security measures added such as higher specification locks. Again, you are under no obligation to provide any extra security assuming the existing provisions meet the required standards. You may choose to fund these extra upgrades yourself or allow the tenant to upgrade at their own costs. Should they decide to install new locks then they should provide the requisite number of keys to you and/or your managing agent. Also, it may be pertinent to ask the tenant to store the old locks for you until the end of the tenancy in case you want to reinstate them.

Your tenant may also want to consider tenant liability insurance which will offer cover in case of damage to your property by the tenant.

INSURANCE SUMMARY

Invest in a landlord's building and contents policy.

Seriously consider the add-ons of cover for incidents where the tenants may need rehousing or where they are not able to pay rent.

Encourage your tenants to get a contents policy and advise why they are valuable as some tenants think the landlord is responsible for damage to their belongings should an accident occur.

NOTES

28

WORKING WITH A MANAGING AGENT

This is not directly related to preparing a property for rental, however, I want to cover it as it is important in relation to some areas of property maintenance.

Managing agents will offer 'let only' services where they find you a tenant for a fee. You then manage the ongoing tenancy.

Agents will also offer fully managed services where they find suitable tenants and manage the tenancy on your behalf throughout the period of the tenancy. This will cost you a management fee, typically 10 to 20 per cent of the monthly rental plus annual renewal fees.

Managing agents will usually manage any repairs on the property through their own contractor base unless you have advised them of your own preferred contractors. This can take the pressure off you but can lead to you not being in direct control of repairs and costs.

One of the major hidden costs when working with a managing agent is the commission related to repairs, where charged. The contractor has to pay the managing agent for the business being passed to them. This is common amongst the larger agents and is usually a percentage of the repair cost.

There are a number of parameters you can put in place to maintain some control over costs when working with a managing agent.

Where reasonable, ask for quotes for works to be done. This is not usually feasible for reactive works with electricians and plumbers and some other contractors who charge for any call-out.

However, for building works such as fencing, roof renovation, and internal redecoration, quotes should be possible.

With mobile phones and the ability to record video and take photos, quotes could be obtained without having to attend the property. This is worth bearing in mind. The process would be to ask the tenant for photos and a video of the issue. Ask them to send them to you and then pass them to a contractor to review.

Be clear about a budget limit for any regular works and allow the agent to carry out works to that amount to cut down excessive communications. This will help avoid you becoming too involved in the tenancy management when you are already paying an agent to do that on your behalf.

You could consider your own team of contractors. This would enable you to control your costs and the quality of the works that are carried out. Working through an agent would still allow you to use your own team. You would need to provide the managing agent property team with your list of contractors, their skillsets, and contacts. Beware that you will need to agree on response times with your team to cater for urgent situations. Advice on this can be sought from the managing agent with respect to accepted lead times. In return, you may want to offer your contractors fast invoice settlement, to keep them loyal.

If working through a managing agent, the agent will need to get express permission from the tenants to pass their contact details over to you or your contractor for repair visits. This should not normally present issues, but you should be aware of this legal requirement.

WORKING WITH A MANAGING AGENT SUMMARY

Prepare clear information for the managing agent about any contractors you want them to use.

Consider a budget for repairs either per repair or per month. This will help to stop you being contacted about small repairs when the managing agent could have just dealt with it.

Ask for quotes where reasonable so that you can consider the best way forward.

NOTES

29

TENANCY DEPOSIT SCHEMES

The tenancy deposit scheme is a system that ensures tenants' deposits are secured for the right reasons. The system also gives you, the landlord, a structured process should you need to call on the deposit for any reason at the end of the tenancy.

A tenancy deposit is effectively an insurance payment by the tenant. In the case of damage to your property, missing or damaged inventory items, or rent arrears at the end of the tenancy, then there are funds you can call on to compensate you.

The tenancy deposit funds must be deposited with one of the authorised services listed below.

The deposit must be set up within 30 days of receipt and the tenant should be notified of the service chosen to hold the deposit.

At the end of the tenancy, the deposit is returned to your tenant unless there are claims to be accounted for. Any claims that you make may be contested by your tenant who may ask the deposit service to adjudicate. Ensure you have all the information and photos you require to back up your claim.

In England, the tenancy deposit is 5 weeks' rent.

In Wales and Northern Ireland, there are no current restrictions.

In Scotland, the tenancy deposit can be up to 2 months' rent.

Choose a deposit service and let your tenant know at check-in which service you will use to caretake their deposit.

England and Wales have 3 schemes:

- The Deposit Protection Service
- Tenancy Deposit Scheme
- MyDeposits

Scotland has 3 schemes:

- Letting Protection Service Scotland
- Safe Deposits Scotland
- MyDeposits Scotland

Northern Ireland has 3 schemes:

- Tenancy Deposit Scheme Northern Ireland
- MyDeposits Northern Ireland
- Letting Protection Service Northern Ireland

TENANCY DEPOSIT SCHEMES SUMMARY

Choose a deposit service and advise the tenant directly or through your managing agent.

Place the money on deposit as soon as you receive it and advise the tenant of the details.

NOTES

30

30: HEALTH AND SAFETY CONSIDERATIONS

This is an area all new landlords need to consider carefully, now more than ever before.

As a landlord you need to develop a risk management mind-set to help look out for potential risks in and around the property that may cause liability. New legislation came into force in 2019. It does not seem to have taken full effect yet, but you should be aware of the objectives of this legislation and ensure you take account of it when planning to rent and manage a property rental. The legislation is the Homes (Fitness for Human Habitation) Act 2018.

This legislation is aimed at raising the standards in private rented housing. Local council environmental departments are the vehicle to manage it in practice.

The headline for the legislation is that rented accommodation needs to be fit for habitation which means that it is safe, healthy, and free from things that could cause serious harm.

There is a 29-point checklist for councils to use to police properties as below.

I am going to discuss some of these risk areas that I have seen come up regularly as issues from tenants.

Damp and mould growth

This is an area you should take very seriously. See the section under Damp. If the tenant believes you are not taking their reporting of damp seriously, this is often an entry point for the local council becoming interested in your property,

Carbon monoxide

I suggest you work ahead of the regulations advised in the section Smoke, Heat, and Carbon Monoxide Alarms. Ensure you install carbon monoxide detectorsfor all relevant gas appliances and check them at the start of the tenancy and replace or repair them when advised that they have failed.

Entry by intruders

See the section on doors and locks. Make sure you meet the minimum standards for security and exceed them, where possible, if you think it will prevent incidents that may have cost implications for you during the tenancy.

Falls associated with stairs and steps

Poorly secured handrails within dwellings and communal stairwells, plus the absence of handrails where it would reduce risk are now recognised as areas that require attention by landlords. Poorly fitted or worn stair carpets are also areas to consider.

Falls on the level

If internal flooring is damaged, such as worn or torn carpeted areas or sheet flooring, then repair these issues before rental. If reported during the tenancy, repair as soon as possible after notification.

Externally, uneven or damaged paving, damaged decking, or even moss-ridden pathways could easily be considered dangerous. Walk the property before rental and check for risks. If you find any, gauge the scale of the potential risk and note for the future, or if you evaluate an issue as high risk, prepare to action remedial works to eliminate the risk prior to the rental.

Electrical hazards

Electrical Installation Condition Reports (EICR) take away much of the risk here, but cabled appliances can sometimes be forgotten, especially if you opt-out of PAT testing. Check appliance cables before tenancy and, where possible, fit plugs to appliances that have a removable fuse fitted on the pin face. This will enable the tenant to change the fuse without having to open the plug which can lead to the cable ends becoming dislodged from their terminals.

Fire and fire safety

Smoke and heat detectorsshould be in place and tested before the tenancy and repaired or replaced in short order if they are identified as faulty during the tenancy.

The full list of 29 hazards that are stipulated in the Act are key focus areas to ensure a property is fit for habitation and are listed below.

If the tenant approaches the environmental health department for a possible breach of the regulations and they take up the case and visit your property then beware that, under the new legislation, the case officer has a duty to check all 29 compliance areas in the property as part of their overall brief.

The government is actively courting the raising of standards in rented accommodation and it is easier to achieve this when they have a reason to visit the property rather than arranging ad hoc appointments with no direct objective.

29 Compliance Areas under the Homes (Fitness for Human Habitation) Act 2018.

1. Damp and mould growth
2. Excess cold
3. Excess heat
4. Asbestos and manufactured metal fibres
5. Biocides (chemicals that treat mould)
6. Carbon monoxide
7. Lead
8. Radiation (from radon gas, which is airborne or in water)
9. Uncombusted fuel gas (leaks in gas appliances)
10. Volatile organic compounds (chemicals which are gases at room temperature)
11. Crowding and space
12. Entry by intruders (such as not having a lock on your front door)
13. Lighting
14. Domestic hygiene, pests, and refuse (including inadequate provision for disposal of wastewater and household waste)

15. Noise
16. Food safety
17. Personal hygiene, sanitation, and drainage
18. Water supply
19. Falls associated with bath or shower
20. Falls associated with stairs and steps
21. Falls on the level (danger of falling on a flat surface)
22. Falls between levels (danger of falling from one level to another, for example, falls out of windows)
23. Electrical hazards
24. Fire and fire safety
25. Hot surfaces and materials
26. Collision and entrapment
27. Explosions
28. Physical strain associated with operating amenities (i.e., very heavy doors)
29. Structural collapse and falling elements

HEALTH AND SAFETY CONSIDERATIONS SUMMARY

Consider carrying out a risk analysis of all the points in the above section.

Going forward, keep in mind that if the local environmental health become involved they are obligated to check all 29 risk categories in your property.

NOTES

31

BLOCK MANAGEMENT COMPANIES FOR FLATS AND APARTMENTS

Should your property be a flat or apartment in a block then there is usually a block management company or entity that will manage the communal areas of the property. They manage the building on behalf of the landlord or freeholder.

They will liaise with the landlord, leaseholders, tenants, and any contractors for issues affecting the communal areas such as gardens, lifts, lighting, fire risk management, etc. Their function is to ensure all services agreed to be provided to the leaseholders are carried out to a satisfactory standard and that the building is kept in good condition.

An area that may help you during the rental period is that the block management company should liaise with flats or apartments where an issue arises in your property that affects another flat or apartment or a communal area. Depending upon the nature of the issue, if damage is caused to the communal area or another flat or apartment, then the claim may be covered by the block management insurance.

BLOCK MANAGEMENT COMPANIES FOR FLATS AND APARTMENTS SUMMARY

Ensure you have the correct management contacts for the management company.

Check the details of the block management insurance policy to see what is covered and in what circumstances.

NOTES

The Energy Crisis Has Guaranteed A Damp Assault On UK Rental Properties In Winter 2022 / 2023!!

READ THIS BOOKLET:

To Understand The Different Types Of Damp

To Find Out Why **Condensation Damp** Is **The Insidious Saboteur!!**

To Understand How **Condensation Damp - The Most Difficult Type Of Damp** Can Be Stopped In Its Tracks By Planning Ahead.

BUT

YOU NEED TO START NOW BEFORE **AUTUMN 2022**

You Need To **Plan Ahead NOW:-**

- If You Want To **Prevent Tenant Complaints**
- If You Want To **Avoid Substantial Remediation Costs**
- If You Want To **Maintain Your Property Asset Value**

Use the QR Code or The Link below To Receive Your Bonus Copy Of Damp The Saboteur condensationmanagement. jamessarsfield.strikepublishing.com

JAMES SARSFIELD
GORDON DREW

CONCLUSION

First, I want to update you about the landlord who suffered that costly leak where there were no stop taps or isolation valves to the sinks, bath, and toilet. He recently added another property to his rental portfolio. He has had a stop tap installed and isolators fitted to all water outlets as part of his investment. Phew!

So, back to business. This book is aimed at the first-time landlord. I hope it has encouraged you to think about what you are about to take on and the different areas you will need to consider as you prepare your property for rental and what ongoing maintenance to plan for whilst it is under tenancy.

Your first task, after reading this book, is to grab a pad and start to pen down the areas that you should tackle with your property to ensure you are in management control of your investment.

Hopefully, you will have made a start by using the 'Notes' pages after each section to help you focus on areas in your property that need attention and have actionable notes. From there, formulate the clauses specific to your property for the tenancy agreement addendum and start to build your Household Management Document.

Even if you are working with a managing agent, you still have your work cut out. Every property is different and managing agents have their own rental format. You will need to provide them with all the management information specific to your property, from shrubs that need regular pruning to your contractor details, and make sure they whistle your tune.

Remember to have a gas check done and then book it annually. The Electrical Installation Condition Report should be done well ahead just in case major works are required which may disrupt wall coverings and flooring. The older the house the more chance works will need to be done to bring the electrical installation up to date.

The next most important are the various emergency detectors that are required. Think strategically about these. Think about management time and safety. Make choices that require the least maintenance and are the most effective. This will bode well for you and your tenants.

The world is going to change for UK landlords in the coming decade.

We will have climate change-induced developments for heating and changing EPC rating targets and ever-increasing pressures to enhance and improve rental properties with new legislation for fire risk reduction and demands coming through from the Habitation Act and pet-related requirements.

Renting is going to become more difficult for landlords with more legislation to adhere to and will, therefore, likely become more expensive for tenants with the upcoming changes needing to be paid for.

I'd like to say you now have all the tools you need but I actually hope I have opened your eyes to at least a couple of areas of which you were not already aware.

I have enjoyed being a landlord and working in the industry. I hope you do too and I wish you all the best.

PLEASE LEAVE A 1-CLICK REVIEW

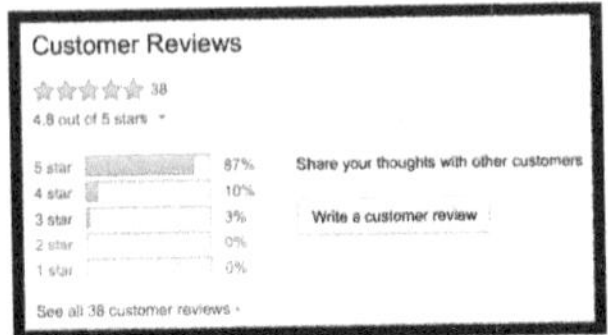

Thank you for buying this book and we sincerely hope you found it valuable.

We will be eternally grateful if you would take just 60 seconds to leave a review.

Below is a 1-click link directly to the Review Page.

Please leave a Star Rating and a short Review.

If you think the book could be improved upon or has omissions or indeed have specific questions about rental property maintenance, please let us know directly by emailing us at info@strikepublishing.com. We will answer every email.

To Leave A Review On The Amazon UK Site Go The Link https://amzn.to/3JKmEpR Or Scan QR Code

For All Other Sites Scroll To 'write A Customer Review'On The Book Sales Page.

GLOSSARY

Annual Gas Check

An annual legal compliance check by a GAS SAFE engineer to ensure all gas appliances and attached flues are safe and safety components are working correctly.

Appliance Check

A process to eliminate each electrical appliance as the cause of a circuit breaker tripping in the consumer unit.

Carbon Monoxide Alarm

A warning device that activates a sound or visible warning in the presence of carbon monoxide that exceeds the recognised safe levels.

Check-In

When a rental property is officially handed over to a tenant at the beginning of the tenancy.

Check-Out

When a rental property is officially handed back to the landlord at the end of a tenancy.

Condensate Pipe

The pipe that takes the water produced during combustion in the boiler to a suitable drain. This pipework may be internal and travel to a suitable internal waste joint or it may be routed externally directly to a drain.

Condensation Damp

The effects of the accumulation of moisture on internal surfaces where bacteria start to grow.

Damp Proof Course

A damp barrier just above ground level to prevent moisture rising up the walls.

Downpipe

The vertical pipe that connects the guttering to the ground drain.

Electrical Installation Condition Report (EICR)

A compliance check that is done every 5 years by a NICEIC or ELECSA approved contractor or a person who holds the technical competence to carry out the test. The electrician will carry out checks on the consumer unit, light fittings, sockets, switches, and cabling to ensure they are safe and working. They will advise what needs changing now and recommend other changes to ensure the installation meets the current electrical standards.

Emergency Control Valve

The red isolation valve on the supply side of the gas meter to switch off the supply in the case of an emergency or the property being vacant for a period.

Energy Performance Certificate (EPC)

An EPC is a certification of how well a property performs in relation to energy and power costs. It will also provide recommendations of improvements to increase energy efficiency and how this will reduce costs to heat or power the property.

Filling Loop

The system built into a boiler or the associated pipework to enable the boiler to be filled with water to re-pressurise it enough to work.

Flashing

The area where the a chimney or other roof structure meets the tiling and has a flexible sheet material to bridge the joint to prevent water ingress at the joint.

Fire-Rated

The standard to which a door is tested to withstand a fire. This may be stated in minutes, for example, FD30 indicates the door is rated to withstand a fire for 30 minutes.

Flat Roof

A roof, usually on an extension, that is flat and often covered in a felting or glass fibre or rubber-based materials.

Freeholder

The person or entity that holds the purchased rights to a property and is also called the landlord.

Grenfell

This name has become synonymous with a major fire that killed 72 people in 2017 and destroyed the block of flats.

Guttering

The horizontal rain collection gulley connected to the house just below the roof line.

Heat Alarm

A warning device that activates a sound or visible warning in the presence of excess heat. These are usually placed in kitchens.

Heating Programmer

A heating programmer allows the heating to be set to go on and off at pre-set times

Heating Thermostat

A heating thermostat is usually installed in the main living space; when the ambient temperature of the room falls below the temperature set on the thermostat it switches the boiler on.

Householder

The person who occupies the property.

Inspection

Periodic checks on the property made by the landlord or his representative to check the status of the property fixtures, fittings, and appliances.

These are property visits aimed at ensuring the property is being managed as expected by the tenant and they enable the landlord to check for any repairs needed and any health and safety issues that may cause future risks.

Inventory

A schedule of inclusions in the rental property that will be included as landlord supplied. The state of the items will be recorded including walls, floors, all fixtures and fittings, and any appliances, etc. This is verified at check-in and check-out. It is possible that this may be done at periodic inspections.

The fixtures, fittings and appliances that come with the tenancy.

Landlord

The person who owns the freehold or leasehold for the rental property.

Leaseholder

The person who holds the rights to the lease and to live or rent out a property for a contracted period of time.

Legionella

Legionella is a bacterium that grows in water systems where the temperature sustains its growth and it causes pneumonia and other respiratory diseases.

Macerator

A unit that takes the debris and water from waste outlets and mechanically breaks it down before it enters the waste pipe to the soil pipe or drain. These are used where waste outlets are added in locations within the property, possibly in extensions.

Magnetic Filter

A component added to a central heating system to remove rusted debris from the system. This makes the system more effective in retaining heat as the cleaner water will absorb more heat from the boiler heat exchanger than dirty, rust-ridden water.

Managing Agent

The company or person who is nominated to manage the rental property during the tenancy. This may include all aspects of the rental from collecting the rent to managing technical issues that arise as well as other tenancy issues.

PIR

A motion sensor system installed in some lights and fans to automatically switch them on.

Pitched Roof

The sloped tiled roof on a property.

Pointing

The cement-based material that is found between bricks.

Portable Appliance Testing (PAT)

A check on any one portable appliance that usually has a cable and plug to check its electrical integrity by visual and electrical checks.

Programmable Room Thermostat

A combined room thermostat and programmer in one unit.

Rising Damp

The effects of moisture ingress at ground level that affect the internal walls. There can be various reasons including a damaged damp proof course.

Skillset

The range of trades or skills used by a contactor or individual.

Sludge

The black water made up of dissolved and rusted metal from the pipework in the central heating system.

Smart Meter

An intelligent device connected to the physical gas or electric meter that sends the readings automatically to the supplier and, via an in-house display, provides information to assist the householder to manage their energy usage.

Smoke Alarm

A warning device that activates a sound or visible warning in the presence of excess smoke from whatever source.

Stop Tap (Stop Cock)

Both of these terms mean a tap that is placed in line with the mains inbound water supply, usually within the property. It enables the householder to isolate the water supply in the case of an emergency or other situation where works may be underway to alter the internal plumbing.

Tenancy

The period you and the tenant agree as the rental period where the tenant has the right to live in the property.

Tenancy Agreement

An agreement between a tenant and a landlord on how the tenancy will be run including rent amount, frequency of payments, and other elements that lay out the legal and other conditions of the tenancy. This can be verbal or a series of emails but it is better in a written format with added conditions or understandings included in an attached addendum.

Tenancy Deposit Scheme

Schemes to lodge tenant deposits to ensure the monies are held in an secure independent space to be returned in full or in part at the end of the tenancy.

Tenant

Person or persons that rent the property for the period of the tenancy.

Thermostatic Control Valve (TCV)

A valve attached to a central heating radiator to detect the room temperature and to allow more hot water into the radiator when the temperature drops below the current setting in the TCV. The valve normally has 5 settings including off to allow effective control of the room temperature.

Thermostatic Radiator Valve (TRV)

A thermostatic radiator valve that enables the temperature of the radiator to be controlled by the flow of hot water into it.

UPVC Windows and Doors

A rigid plastic material used to manufacture windows and doors.

RESOURCES

Tenancy:

https://www.gov.uk/government/publications/model-agreement-for-a-shorthold-assured-tenancy

Property Boundaries:

https://www.gov.uk/your-property-boundaries

Doors:

https://www.london-fire.gov.uk/safety/property-management/fire-doors/

Locks:

https://www.landlordstudio.com/blog/whats-the-best-lock-for-a-rental-property/

Electrical Installations:

https://www.nrla.org.uk/resources/looking-after-your-property/electrical-safety-inspections

PAT Testing:

https://www.hse.gov.uk/electricity/faq-portable-appliance-testing.htm

Emergency Detectors:

https://www.gov.uk/government/publications/smoke-and-carbon-monoxide-alarms-explanatory-booklet-for-landlords

https://www.mygov.scot/home-fire-safety

https://sheltercymru.org.uk/get-advice/repairs-and-bad-conditions/home-safety/fire-safety-responsibilities/

https://www.nidirect.gov.uk/articles/smoke-alarms-and-fire-emergency-equipment

Fire Safety:

https://www.gov.uk/government/publications/fire-safety-in-purpose-built-blocks-of-flats

Smart Meters:

https://www.gov.uk/guidance/smart-meters-how-they-work

Gas and Heating:

https://www.hse.gov.uk/gas/landlords/safetycheckswho.htm

https://www.britishgas.co.uk/home-services/landlords/gas-safety-need-to-know.html

Damp:

https://www.which.co.uk/reviews/damp/article/damp/what-kind-of-damp-is-affecting-my-home-arNnf1P2wVnV

https://energysavingtrust.org.uk/advice/fixing-damp-and-condensation/

Pets:

https://www.gov.uk/government/news/new-standard-tenancy-agreement-to-help-renters-with-well-behaved-pets

https://www.letswithpets.org.uk/news-and-updates/news-and-updates-1

Insurance:

https://www.gov.uk/renting-out-a-property

Tenancy Deposit Schemes:

https://www.gov.uk/tenancy-deposit-protection

https://www.mygov.scot/tenancy-deposits-landlords

https://sheltercymru.org.uk/get-advice/paying-for-housing/tenancy-deposits/tenancy-deposit-protection-schemes/

https://www.nidirect.gov.uk/information-and-services/private-renting/tenancy-deposit-scheme

Homes Act 2018:

https://www.gov.uk/government/publications/homes-fitness-for-human-habitation-act-2018/guide-for-landlords-homes-fitness-for-human-habitation-act-2018

Energy Performance:

https://www.gov.uk/guidance/apply-for-the-green-homes-grant-scheme

Made in the USA
Coppell, TX
17 October 2022

84777154R00138